Account Based Marketing Complete Self-Assessment Guide

The guidance in this Self-Assessment is based on Account Based Marketing best practices and standards in business process architecture, design and quality management. The guidance is also based on the professional judgment of the individual collaborators listed in the Acknowledgments.

http://theartofservice.com
service@theartofservice.com

Table of Contents

About The Art of Service

The Art of Service, Business Process Architects since 2000, is dedicated to helping stakeholders achieve excellence.

Defining, designing, creating, and implementing a process to solve a stakeholders challenge or meet an objective is the most valuable role… In EVERY group, company, organization and department.

Unless you're talking a one-time, single-use project, there should be a process. Whether that process is managed and implemented by humans, AI, or a combination of the two, it needs to be designed by someone with a complex enough perspective to ask the right questions.

Someone capable of asking the right questions and step back and say, 'What are we really trying to accomplish here? And is there a different way to look at it?'

With The Art of Service's Standard Requirements Self-Assessments, we empower people who can do just that — whether their title is marketer, entrepreneur, manager, salesperson, consultant, Business Process Manager, executive assistant, IT Manager, CIO etc... —they are the people who rule the future. They are people who watch the process as it happens, and ask the right questions to make the process work better.

Contact us when you need any support with this Self-Assessment and any help with templates, blue-prints and examples of standard documents you might need:

http://theartofservice.com
service@theartofservice.com

Included Resources - how to access

Included with your purchase of the book is the Account Based

Marketing Self-Assessment Spreadsheet Dashboard which contains all questions and Self-Assessment areas and auto-generates insights, graphs, and project RACI planning - all with examples to get you started right away.

How? Simply send an email to
access@theartofservice.com
with this books' title in the subject to get the Account Based Marketing Self Assessment Tool right away.

You will receive the following contents with New and Updated specific criteria:

- The latest quick edition of the book in PDF
- The latest complete edition of the book in PDF, which criteria correspond to the criteria in...
- The Self-Assessment Excel Dashboard, and...
- Example pre-filled Self-Assessment Excel Dashboard to get familiar with results generation
- In-depth specific Checklists covering the topic
- Project management checklists and templates to assist with implementation

INCLUDES LIFETIME SELF ASSESSMENT UPDATES

Every self assessment comes with Lifetime Updates and Lifetime Free Updated Books. Lifetime Updates is an industry-first feature which allows you to receive verified self assessment updates, ensuring you always have the most accurate information at your fingertips.

Get it now- you will be glad you did - do it now, before you forget.

Send an email to **access@theartofservice.com** with this books' title in the subject to get the Account Based Marketing Self Assessment Tool right away.

Purpose of this Self-Assessment

This Self-Assessment has been developed to improve understanding of the requirements and elements of Account Based Marketing, based on best practices and standards in business process architecture, design and quality management.

It is designed to allow for a rapid Self-Assessment to determine how closely existing management practices and procedures correspond to the elements of the Self-Assessment.

The criteria of requirements and elements of Account Based Marketing have been rephrased in the format of a Self-Assessment questionnaire, with a seven-criterion scoring system, as explained in this document.

In this format, even with limited background knowledge of Account Based Marketing, a manager can quickly review existing operations to determine how they measure up to the standards. This in turn can serve as the starting point of a 'gap analysis' to identify management tools or system elements that might usefully be implemented in the organization to help improve overall performance.

How to use the Self-Assessment

On the following pages are a series of questions to identify to what extent your Account Based Marketing initiative is complete in comparison to the requirements set in standards.

To facilitate answering the questions, there is a space in front of each question to enter a score on a scale of '1' to '5'.

1 Strongly Disagree

2 Disagree

3 Neutral

4 Agree

5 Strongly Agree

Read the question and rate it with the following in front of mind:

**'In my belief,
the answer to this question is clearly defined'.**

There are two ways in which you can choose to interpret this statement;

1. how aware are you that the answer to the question is clearly defined
2. for more in-depth analysis you can choose to gather evidence and confirm the answer to the question. This obviously will take more time, most Self-Assessment users opt for the first way to interpret the question and dig deeper later on based on the outcome of the overall Self-Assessment.

A score of '1' would mean that the answer is not clear at all, where a '5' would mean the answer is crystal clear and defined. Leave emtpy when the question is not applicable or you don't want to answer it, you can skip it without affecting your score. Write your score in the space provided.

After you have responded to all the appropriate statements in each section, compute your average score for that section, using the formula provided, and round to the nearest tenth. Then transfer to the corresponding spoke in the Account Based Marketing Scorecard on the second next page of the Self-Assessment.

Your completed Account Based Marketing Scorecard will give you a clear presentation of which Account Based Marketing areas need attention.

Account Based Marketing Scorecard Example

Example of how the finalized Scorecard can look like:

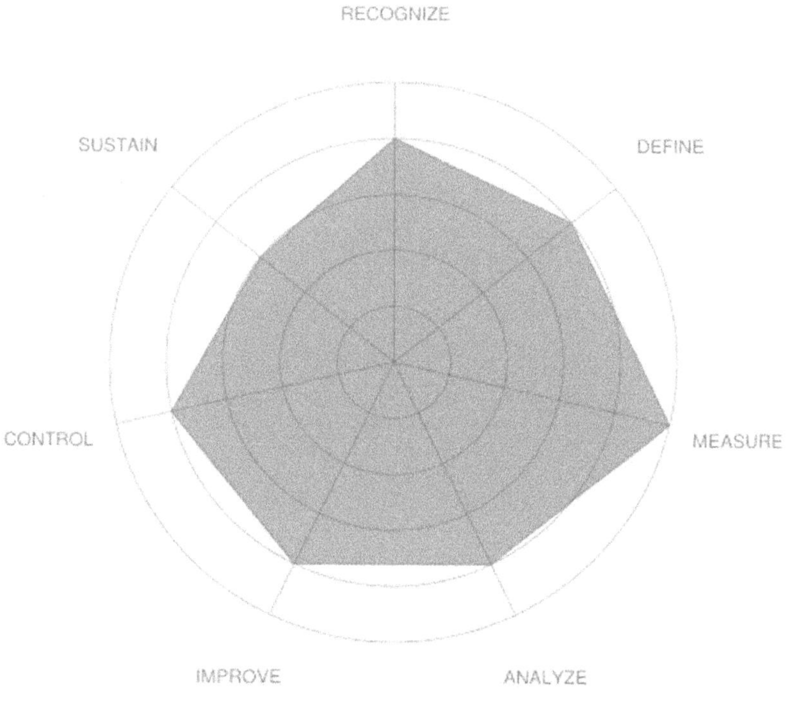

Account Based Marketing Scorecard

Your Scores:

BEGINNING OF THE SELF-ASSESSMENT:

CRITERION #1: RECOGNIZE

INTENT: Be aware of the need for change. Recognize that there is an unfavorable variation, problem or symptom.

In my belief, the answer to this question is clearly defined:

5 Strongly Agree

4 Agree

3 Neutral

2 Disagree

1 Strongly Disagree

1. What kind of marketing automation toolset do you need?
<--- Score

2. Time is money. How much implementation time will you need to invest to get this up and running?
<--- Score

3. Final point to consider before you start

comparing vendors: What other tools will your marketing automation system need to integrate with?
<--- Score

4. Why do you need marketing automation?
<--- Score

5. Do you need more web traffic from your target accounts?
<--- Score

6. What skills are most needed today in PR and marketing?
<--- Score

7. Do you have all the tools and resources you need to start building your strategy?
<--- Score

8. What kind of third-party vendors will you need for your event?
<--- Score

9. Is a crm tool what you really need?
<--- Score

10. What are the current systems in place that need to interact with the automation system?
<--- Score

11. Which factors need to be considered to achieve success with viral marketing campaign?
<--- Score

12. Do you receive the level of support you need?

<--- Score

13. Play nicely. what are the current systems in place that need to interact with the automation system?
<--- Score

14. What kind of marketing automation platform do you need?
<--- Score

15. What problem does it solve?
<--- Score

16. What things need to change to make sales more effective?
<--- Score

17. Does your organization need a marketing automation tool?
<--- Score

18. What potential problems may complicate test marketing?
<--- Score

19. Does the cmo need to sign off on all marketing contracts?
<--- Score

20. What business problems do you solve?
<--- Score

21. At what point in your sales cycle do your prospects need to be followed up and at what intervals?

<--- Score

22. Does it include the features you need?
<--- Score

23. What pricing tactics will be used initially or eventually?
<--- Score

24. What are the stakeholder objectives to be achieved with Account-Based Marketing?
<--- Score

25. Does your organization need a marketing automation platform?
<--- Score

26. How do you attract the leads you need to grow your business?
<--- Score

27. As a sponsor, customer or management, how important is it to meet goals, objectives?
<--- Score

28. Is there increasing recognition that agility is an imperative for success of your organization as it faces intense rivalry, globalization, and time-to-market pressures?
<--- Score

29. What would happen if Account-Based Marketing weren't done?
<--- Score

30. What are the expected benefits of Account-Based

Marketing to the stakeholder?
<--- Score

31. What does Account-Based Marketing success mean to the stakeholders?
<--- Score

32. What are the guidelines for effective brand-building events and experiences in your organization?
<--- Score

33. How do marketing and sales work to identify and select target accounts?
<--- Score

34. Do you need a marketing automation system?
<--- Score

35. In building the marketing automation stack, who needs what?
<--- Score

36. What questions do you need to answer?
<--- Score

37. Marketing objective: what problem do you hope to solve?
<--- Score

38. Is your business/product recognized by the target market?
<--- Score

39. Are there any specific expectations or concerns about the Account-Based Marketing team, Account-

Based Marketing itself?
<--- Score

40. How much content do you need to get started with marketing automation?
<--- Score

41. How much are sponsors, customers, partners, stakeholders involved in Account-Based Marketing? In other words, what are the risks, if Account-Based Marketing does not deliver successfully?
<--- Score

42. Do you have a business need to use flows outside of a console app?
<--- Score

43. Do they need to download an asset, click on a CTA, or take no action on an email?
<--- Score

44. What do you really need to know about marketing automation before you buy?
<--- Score

45. What is needed to actually manage multichannel marketing campaigns and one-to-one interactions with customers around the clock?
<--- Score

46. What are the key issues with e-commerce and m-commerce?
<--- Score

47. How does it meet the business needs in a streamlined fashion?

<--- Score

48. How are you going to measure success?
<--- Score

49. What situation(s) led to this Account-Based Marketing Self Assessment?
<--- Score

50. What is the problem you are trying to solve?
<--- Score

51. What business problem/s do you want to resolve?
<--- Score

52. What is needed to manage multichannel marketing campaigns and one-to-one interactions with customers around the clock?
<--- Score

53. Who else hopes to benefit from it?
<--- Score

54. What if your marketing systems are down when your event is just about to start?
<--- Score

55. What problems are you facing and how do you consider Account-Based Marketing will circumvent those obstacles?
<--- Score

56. What kind of marketing automation tools do you need?
<--- Score

57. What is the business functionality that needs to be delivered?
<--- Score

58. What kind of marketing automation tool do you need?
<--- Score

59. Are there any existing systems that the new system will need to integrate with?
<--- Score

60. What do marketing automation vendors and customers alike need to push marketing automation maturity to the next level?
<--- Score

61. Do you need a fully integrated marketing automation system to support you?
<--- Score

62. How are the Account-Based Marketing's objectives aligned to the group's overall stakeholder strategy?
<--- Score

63. Have you had any maintenance issues with the system?
<--- Score

64. How can it meet the business needs in a streamlined fashion?
<--- Score

Add up total points for this section:
_____ = Total points for this section

Divided by: ______ (number of statements answered) = ______ Average score for this section

Transfer your score to the Account-Based Marketing Index at the beginning of the Self-Assessment.

CRITERION #2: DEFINE:

INTENT: Formulate the stakeholder problem. Define the problem, needs and objectives.

In my belief, the answer to this question is clearly defined:

5 Strongly Agree

4 Agree

3 Neutral

2 Disagree

1 Strongly Disagree

1. How can you create a quantitative business case for faster revenue growth?
<--- Score

2. Is the current 'as is' process being followed? If not, what are the discrepancies?
<--- Score

3. Is there a Account-Based Marketing management

charter, including stakeholder case, problem and goal statements, scope, milestones, roles and responsibilities, communication plan?
<--- Score

4. How does the Account-Based Marketing manager ensure against scope creep?
<--- Score

5. What are the rough order estimates on cost savings/ opportunities that Account-Based Marketing brings?
<--- Score

6. What would be the goal or target for a Account-Based Marketing's improvement team?
<--- Score

7. Is a fully trained team formed, supported, and committed to work on the Account-Based Marketing improvements?
<--- Score

8. Are customer(s) identified and segmented according to their different needs and requirements?
<--- Score

9. What reporting requirements do you have?
<--- Score

10. Has anyone else (internal or external to the group) attempted to solve this problem or a similar one before? If so, what knowledge can be leveraged from these previous efforts?
<--- Score

11. Will team members perform Account-Based

Marketing work when assigned and in a timely fashion?
<--- Score

12. When is/was the Account-Based Marketing start date?
<--- Score

13. What customer feedback methods were used to solicit their input?
<--- Score

14. Are different versions of process maps needed to account for the different types of inputs?
<--- Score

15. How should ethical corporate marketing be defined?
<--- Score

16. Is Account-Based Marketing currently on schedule according to the plan?
<--- Score

17. Who are the Account-Based Marketing improvement team members, including Management Leads and Coaches?
<--- Score

18. How is the team tracking and documenting its work?
<--- Score

19. How was the 'as is' process map developed, reviewed, verified and validated?
<--- Score

20. Is there a critical path to deliver Account-Based Marketing results?
<--- Score

21. Has the Account-Based Marketing work been fairly and/or equitably divided and delegated among team members who are qualified and capable to perform the work? Has everyone contributed?
<--- Score

22. Do the problem and goal statements meet the SMART criteria (specific, measurable, attainable, relevant, and time-bound)?
<--- Score

23. What critical content must be communicated – who, what, when, where, and how?
<--- Score

24. Is the team sponsored by a champion or stakeholder leader?
<--- Score

25. Is there regularly 100% attendance at the team meetings? If not, have appointed substitutes attended to preserve cross-functionality and full representation?
<--- Score

26. Will there be other use cases from a marketing outreach perspective for sending communication to customers?
<--- Score

27. What are the compelling stakeholder reasons for

embarking on Account-Based Marketing?
<--- Score

28. Is full participation by members in regularly held team meetings guaranteed?
<--- Score

29. Has a project plan, Gantt chart, or similar been developed/completed?
<--- Score

30. How do you keep key subject matter experts in the loop?
<--- Score

31. Has a team charter been developed and communicated?
<--- Score

32. When is the estimated completion date?
<--- Score

33. Has a high-level 'as is' process map been completed, verified and validated?
<--- Score

34. Is the team equipped with available and reliable resources?
<--- Score

35. Are there different segments of customers?
<--- Score

36. Are stakeholder processes mapped?
<--- Score

37. Is data collected and displayed to better understand customer(s) critical needs and requirements.
<--- Score

38. What are the requirements for successful ingredient branding?
<--- Score

39. Are customers identified and high impact areas defined?
<--- Score

40. What are the requirements for effective segmentation?
<--- Score

41. Are improvement team members fully trained on Account-Based Marketing?
<--- Score

42. Is the team adequately staffed with the desired cross-functionality? If not, what additional resources are available to the team?
<--- Score

43. Is the team formed and are team leaders (Coaches and Management Leads) assigned?
<--- Score

44. Are team charters developed?
<--- Score

45. What are the boundaries of the scope? What is in bounds and what is not? What is the start point? What is the stop point?

<--- Score

46. What are barriers to success in creating a valid business case?
<--- Score

47. What 3rd party systems will be required to integrate and how many there are?
<--- Score

48. What key stakeholder process output measure(s) does Account-Based Marketing leverage and how?
<--- Score

49. When are meeting minutes sent out? Who is on the distribution list?
<--- Score

50. What constraints exist that might impact the team?
<--- Score

51. How will variation in the actual durations of each activity be dealt with to ensure that the expected Account-Based Marketing results are met?
<--- Score

52. How do you discover and define your target accounts?
<--- Score

53. What specifically is the problem? Where does it occur? When does it occur? What is its extent?
<--- Score

54. Are there any constraints known that bear on the

ability to perform Account-Based Marketing work? How is the team addressing them?
<--- Score

55. Has/have the customer(s) been identified?
<--- Score

56. How do you define the market, how big is it, and how fast is it growing?
<--- Score

57. Has the direction changed at all during the course of Account-Based Marketing? If so, when did it change and why?
<--- Score

58. What are the dynamics of the communication plan?
<--- Score

59. Is there a completed, verified, and validated high-level 'as is' (not 'should be' or 'could be') stakeholder process map?
<--- Score

60. Have the customer needs been translated into specific, measurable requirements? How?
<--- Score

61. Is the Account-Based Marketing scope manageable?
<--- Score

62. How often are the team meetings?
<--- Score

63. Is there a completed SIPOC representation, describing the Suppliers, Inputs, Process, Outputs, and Customers?
<--- Score

64. What are the Roles and Responsibilities for each team member and its leadership? Where is this documented?
<--- Score

65. Will team members regularly document their Account-Based Marketing work?
<--- Score

66. Is the improvement team aware of the different versions of a process: what they think it is vs. what it actually is vs. what it should be vs. what it could be?
<--- Score

67. How will the Account-Based Marketing team and the group measure complete success of Account-Based Marketing?
<--- Score

68. Is Account-Based Marketing linked to key stakeholder goals and objectives?
<--- Score

69. How much IT effort is required to implement marketing automation?
<--- Score

70. If substitutes have been appointed, have they been briefed on the Account-Based Marketing goals and received regular communications as to the progress to date?

<--- Score

71. Has the improvement team collected the 'voice of the customer' (obtained feedback – qualitative and quantitative)?
<--- Score

72. Does the team have regular meetings?
<--- Score

73. How did the Account-Based Marketing manager receive input to the development of a Account-Based Marketing improvement plan and the estimated completion dates/times of each activity?
<--- Score

74. What actions does implementing marketing automation require when thinking of human resources?
<--- Score

75. Will there be several use cases from a marketing outreach perspective for sending communication to customers?
<--- Score

76. Has everyone on the team, including the team leaders, been properly trained?
<--- Score

Add up total points for this section:
_____ = Total points for this section

Divided by: ______ (number of statements answered) = ______
Average score for this section

Transfer your score to the Account-Based Marketing Index at the beginning of the Self-Assessment.

CRITERION #3: MEASURE:

INTENT: Gather the correct data. Measure the current performance and evolution of the situation.

In my belief, the answer to this question is clearly defined:

5 Strongly Agree

4 Agree

3 Neutral

2 Disagree

1 Strongly Disagree

1. Are process variation components displayed/ communicated using suitable charts, graphs, plots?
<--- Score

2. How does your organization use RPA to reach the right customers, cut marketing costs, and increase sales?
<--- Score

3. What sort of impact has marketing automation had on you and your team?
<--- Score

4. Was a data collection plan established?
<--- Score

5. Will you help you define and prioritize business processes as preparation for the final utilization of the marketing automation platform?
<--- Score

6. What new features are you focusing on for the coming year?
<--- Score

7. Where do you focus your marketing and promotion efforts?
<--- Score

8. What charts has the team used to display the components of variation in the process?
<--- Score

9. How reliable is the data analysis?
<--- Score

10. How much does it cost you to acquire a customer?
<--- Score

11. What types of issues can impact the marketing and sales organization during an M&A transaction?
<--- Score

12. Is long term and short term variability accounted for?
<--- Score

13. Have you found any 'ground fruit' or 'low-hanging fruit' for immediate remedies to the gap in performance?
<--- Score

14. Is there a Performance Baseline?
<--- Score

15. What data sources have you seen combined with web analytics and the core marketing data sources?
<--- Score

16. Who participated in the data collection for measurements?
<--- Score

17. What particular quality tools did the team find helpful in establishing measurements?
<--- Score

18. Which are likely to be your organizations top business priorities over the next 12 months?
<--- Score

19. What should you focus on when selling marketing automation to your executive team?
<--- Score

20. What is the cost of marketing automation?
<--- Score

21. Within your organization, where do you expect AI to have the greatest impact?
<--- Score

22. How does ai impact account-based marketing?
<--- Score

23. Is key measure data collection planned and executed, process variation displayed and communicated and performance baselined?
<--- Score

24. Is data collected on key measures that were identified?
<--- Score

25. What costs are missing to fully account for data-based information?
<--- Score

26. How do you measure the payback from advertising, sales promotion, and public relations?
<--- Score

27. What key measures identified indicate the performance of the stakeholder process?
<--- Score

28. What kind of reports does the marketing automation platform provide for leads, email programs, campaign results and web analytics?
<--- Score

29. How do you measure the effectiveness of your marketing?
<--- Score

30. Is Process Variation Displayed/Communicated?
<--- Score

31. How large is the gap between current performance and the customer-specified (goal) performance?
<--- Score

32. How do you measure the effect of social media marketing on your business?
<--- Score

33. What data should marketers prioritize?
<--- Score

34. How will marketing and sales be measured on activities and impact?
<--- Score

35. How long does it take to analyze campaign data across all marketing channels without a marketing automation system?
<--- Score

36. How do you select and prioritize your accounts using the data-driven approach?
<--- Score

37. What has the team done to assure the stability and accuracy of the measurement process?
<--- Score

38. How do you measure brand equity?
<--- Score

39. In which other countries do you provide local support, with knowledge of local laws that could impact your marketing efforts?
<--- Score

40. What are key strategic priorities for the accounts you are targeting?
<--- Score

41. Do you want to evolve your marketing analytics strategy so that its built for long-term success?
<--- Score

42. What are the agreed upon definitions of the high impact areas, defect(s), unit(s), and opportunities that will figure into the process capability metrics?
<--- Score

43. Do you analyze your data and reporting on KPIs and ROI?
<--- Score

44. How much does it cost to bring a product to the market?
<--- Score

45. Will this knowledge have an impact on your marketing strategies?
<--- Score

46. Is a solid data collection plan established that includes measurement systems analysis?
<--- Score

47. What data was collected (past, present, future/

ongoing)?
<--- Score

48. What do you need to focus on, how will this be measured and which tools meet such requirements?
<--- Score

49. How will you measure success?
<--- Score

50. Are key measures identified and agreed upon?
<--- Score

51. Are the integrations expected to be in the implementation cost?
<--- Score

52. How can you maintain margins while enduring intense price pressure and spiraling costs?
<--- Score

53. How much does it cost to hire your sales and marketing team?
<--- Score

54. Is data collection planned and executed?
<--- Score

55. Do you have the ability to look at a list of potential customers and prioritize them based on t with your business and likelihood to buy?
<--- Score

56. What are the key input variables? What are the key process variables? What are the key output variables?

<--- Score

57. What is the cost benefit ratio for the data analysis effort?
<--- Score

58. Is your organization investing in Dark Data Analytics?
<--- Score

59. How much does marketing automation cost?
<--- Score

60. Do sales and marketing focus on that same list of target accounts?
<--- Score

61. Are high impact defects defined and identified in the stakeholder process?
<--- Score

Add up total points for this section:
_____ = Total points for this section

Divided by: ______ (number of statements answered) = ______ Average score for this section

Transfer your score to the Account-Based Marketing Index at the beginning of the Self-Assessment.

CRITERION #4: ANALYZE:

INTENT: Analyze causes, assumptions and hypotheses.

In my belief, the answer to this question is clearly defined:

5 Strongly Agree

4 Agree

3 Neutral

2 Disagree

1 Strongly Disagree

1. What did the team gain from developing a sub-process map?
<--- Score

2. How will your data be managed?
<--- Score

3. What major changes are occurring in product and process technology?
<--- Score

4. Is the performance gap determined?
<--- Score

5. Is the gap/opportunity displayed and communicated in financial terms?
<--- Score

6. What data should you be collecting?
<--- Score

7. Does anyone review the data?
<--- Score

8. Do you need a customer data platform?
<--- Score

9. Where do you begin with your approach to data integrity?
<--- Score

10. Is data and process analysis, root cause analysis and quantifying the gap/opportunity in place?
<--- Score

11. What kind of data can you generate?
<--- Score

12. As marketers come and go, how are you going to steward the processes and data you need to operate?
<--- Score

13. What were the crucial 'moments of truth' on the process map?
<--- Score

14. How does customer loyalty translate into account growth and upsell opportunity?
<--- Score

15. Does it require extensive data clean up to integrate?
<--- Score

16. How does content marketing change in a Data Lake environment?
<--- Score

17. Which processes do you currently have established between your Sales and Marketing teams?
<--- Score

18. How long does it take to qualify, score, and assign prospects without a marketing automation system?
<--- Score

19. Are data collected over time?
<--- Score

20. Is one type of data more valuable than another?
<--- Score

21. What is marketing automation and how does it differ from other digital marketing processes?
<--- Score

22. Can you generate data from the program in a way that gives you a holistic view of performance?

<--- Score

23. Where will your data be stored?
<--- Score

24. Get unstuck. what are your current lead management processes and where are the speci c areas you would like to automate?
<--- Score

25. Is it easy to share your data throughout your organization?
<--- Score

26. What is the volume of data that is to be migrated into the new solution?
<--- Score

27. Was a cause-and-effect diagram used to explore the different types of causes (or sources of variation)?
<--- Score

28. What quality tools were used to get through the analyze phase?
<--- Score

29. How will your data be secured?
<--- Score

30. How good is your data?
<--- Score

31. Did any value-added analysis or 'lean thinking' take place to identify some of the gaps shown on the 'as is' process map?
<--- Score

32. What does the data say about the performance of the stakeholder process?
<--- Score

33. Are you able to automate the deletion of customer data?
<--- Score

34. Is it possible to encrypt data?
<--- Score

35. How do consumers process and evaluate your prices?
<--- Score

36. Are you using the right data to make the right actionable decisions?
<--- Score

37. What tools, technologies and data structures already exist across your organization?
<--- Score

38. What is the future of the Marketing Data Lake?
<--- Score

39. Is aggregated data by time period available?
<--- Score

40. Is marketing responsible for a sales-qualified lead goal?
<--- Score

41. How does data-driven decision making affect your organizations performance?

<--- Score

42. Customer data platform or marketing automation what do you really need?
<--- Score

43. Was a detailed process map created to amplify critical steps of the 'as is' stakeholder process?
<--- Score

44. Has your marketing automation system and data grown into an unruly mess?
<--- Score

45. How easy is it to customize the system to your specific business model and/or sales process?
<--- Score

46. Review leads with high scores that did not turn into opportunities. How could the scoring be improved?
<--- Score

47. Where does the data from your customer base reside now?
<--- Score

48. When is customer data on the marketing cloud ftp deleted?
<--- Score

49. What is the cost of poor quality as supported by the team's analysis?
<--- Score

50. Which areas of your marketing and sales

processes could be more efficient?
<--- Score

51. How easy is it to customize the system to your specific business model and/ or sales process?
<--- Score

52. Is there an annual membership or similar which is processed through another system?
<--- Score

53. What does it mean to master data and in the process maximize your account-based marketing?
<--- Score

54. Is digital data-based information an asset?
<--- Score

55. Are there specific reasons for various pieces of data that are collected?
<--- Score

56. Where is data stored and who is responsible for ensuring that the data is collected?
<--- Score

57. Do you have the necessary data points to drive your segmentation?
<--- Score

58. How can you use Computer Profile data for direct marketing and be GDPR-compliant?
<--- Score

59. What if your data changes with the seasons?
<--- Score

60. Opportunities by industry - what types of opportunities are available from various industries?
<--- Score

61. Are gaps between current performance and the goal performance identified?
<--- Score

62. What were the key business processes and goals you set for this marketing automation project?
<--- Score

63. What drives packaging innovation?
<--- Score

64. Can print and mail be part of the marketing automation process?
<--- Score

65. Where is the data recorded?
<--- Score

66. While there are a lot of other things to consider further down in the decision-making process, first consider: What are you trying to achieve?
<--- Score

67. How does the consumer process competitive brand information and make a final value judgment?
<--- Score

68. If you do not have a clear understanding of

what types of data should be in your database, how can you expect it to provide optimal value?
<--- Score

69. How does a marketing organization become more data driven?
<--- Score

70. How do you implement a data-driven account based marketing strategy in your business today?
<--- Score

71. What tools were used to narrow the list of possible causes?
<--- Score

72. How will you use this data?
<--- Score

73. Which variables are the key drivers of choice in a market?
<--- Score

74. Roles and responsibilities: who will be accountable and responsible for activities in marketing processes?
<--- Score

75. Is the data lake for everyone?
<--- Score

76. Do you aggregate and mine data to provide a summary of historical data that answers: What has happened?
<--- Score

77. Also consider missed opportunities right in front of you where you already have the active attention of your target audience. How can you maximize is?
<--- Score

78. How are you going to clean and enrich your data?
<--- Score

79. What was selling like before the big data marketing program?
<--- Score

80. What data do you already have?
<--- Score

81. How do you relate transactional data to marketing?
<--- Score

82. Where do you put all this data?
<--- Score

83. What items do you need to provide to the prospect during the sales process?
<--- Score

84. How old is the data?
<--- Score

85. What tools were used to generate the list of possible causes?
<--- Score

86. Do you struggle with duplicate data in your

current system of record?
<--- Score

87. Is the Account-Based Marketing process severely broken such that a re-design is necessary?
<--- Score

88. If you are using marketing automation, how does this help to enhance the digital marketing actions and what processes are automated?
<--- Score

89. What are your current lead management processes and where are the specific areas you would like to automate?
<--- Score

90. What were the financial benefits resulting from any 'ground fruit or low-hanging fruit' (quick fixes)?
<--- Score

91. Why is it so important that Marketing and Sales Development work together throughout the buying process?
<--- Score

92. What major psychological processes influence consumer responses to the marketing program?
<--- Score

93. How do you become proficient in designing and implementing marketing workflows that drive your organizations business?
<--- Score

94. Do you have enough contacts in your target

accounts in your database?
<--- Score

95. Did any additional data need to be collected?
<--- Score

96. What are paper or hard copy based processes affected by this project?
<--- Score

97. Do you need to modify your end-to-end business revenue process and/or improve marketing-sales alignment?
<--- Score

98. How do consumers perceive data ownership and privacy in a time of Big Data?
<--- Score

99. What approach is used to migrate years of activity data from your legacy marketing automation platform to the new platform?
<--- Score

100. Is your marketing team responsible for a sales-qualified lead goal?
<--- Score

101. Is the data clean and consistent?
<--- Score

102. What are your top pain points when it comes to developing or refining your data-driven marketing strategy?
<--- Score

103. What are the revised rough estimates of the financial savings/opportunity for Account-Based Marketing improvements?
<--- Score

104. Were there any improvement opportunities identified from the process analysis?
<--- Score

105. Were any designed experiments used to generate additional insight into the data analysis?
<--- Score

106. Opportunities by category - what types of opportunities are available by category?
<--- Score

107. How data-driven is your marketing organization?
<--- Score

108. Were Pareto charts (or similar) used to portray the 'heavy hitters' (or key sources of variation)?
<--- Score

109. What organizational structures and processes do managers use to oversee new-product development?
<--- Score

110. Do you have data in a variety of sources and are unsure of how to draw conclusions?
<--- Score

111. The best companies make data-driven decisions to drive sales and marketing efforts.

Are you using the right data to make the right actionable decisions?
<--- Score

112. How was the detailed process map generated, verified, and validated?
<--- Score

113. How much data does a customer produce?
<--- Score

114. Do you collect customer data in multiple systems?
<--- Score

115. Have any additional benefits been identified that will result from closing all or most of the gaps?
<--- Score

116. What conclusions were drawn from the team's data collection and analysis? How did the team reach these conclusions?
<--- Score

117. How will your data get cleansed – and maintained – to ensure your marketing automation does not suffer from garbage in, garbage out?
<--- Score

118. How many opportunities did marketing generate?
<--- Score

119. Is there an annual membership or similar which is processed?

<--- Score

120. How do you identify and evaluate market opportunities?
<--- Score

121. How can an Administrator find the number of mailable prospects in database?
<--- Score

122. Do you have sufficient data and contacts for each target account?
<--- Score

123. Does the marketing automation system support an automated mapping of your data model?
<--- Score

124. Have the problem and goal statements been updated to reflect the additional knowledge gained from the analyze phase?
<--- Score

125. Opportunities by type - what types of opportunities are available by type?
<--- Score

126. Is your data segmented anywhere?
<--- Score

127. What is the process for utilizing the customer journey in marketing automation?
<--- Score

128. Can lead scoring be based on activity data in

the CRM?
<--- Score

129. What data do you have?
<--- Score

Add up total points for this section:
_____ = Total points for this section

Divided by: ______ (number of statements answered) = ______ Average score for this section

Transfer your score to the Account-Based Marketing Index at the beginning of the Self-Assessment.

CRITERION #5: IMPROVE:

INTENT: Develop a practical solution. Innovate, establish and test the solution and to measure the results.

In my belief, the answer to this question is clearly defined:

5 Strongly Agree

4 Agree

3 Neutral

2 Disagree

1 Strongly Disagree

1. Are improved process ('should be') maps modified based on pilot data and analysis?
<--- Score

2. What is your commitment to R&D as a percentage of your total expenditure dedicated to improvements?
<--- Score

3. How can you combine different types of content with marketing automation for the best results?
<--- Score

4. Care and feeding. As with any technology, marketing automation tools evolve. Who is going to own it and ensure that its being optimized?
<--- Score

5. Are the target accounts aware of your organization and its solutions?
<--- Score

6. How do you optimize marketing automation to continually increase performance?
<--- Score

7. What lessons, if any, from a pilot were incorporated into the design of the full-scale solution?
<--- Score

8. Which marketing automation platform (map) do you use?
<--- Score

9. How do consumers make purchasing decisions?
<--- Score

10. What are the risks of marketing automation?
<--- Score

11. Are new and improved process ('should be') maps developed?
<--- Score

12. What is Account-Based Marketing's impact on

utilizing the best solution(s)?
<--- Score

13. Is a solution implementation plan established, including schedule/work breakdown structure, resources, risk management plan, cost/budget, and control plan?
<--- Score

14. Is there a cost/benefit analysis of optimal solution(s)?
<--- Score

15. What have been the results and where has it been used?
<--- Score

16. How will the group know that the solution worked?
<--- Score

17. What decisions does your organization face in managing channels?
<--- Score

18. Each of the areas will need to be developed towards the outcome that has been decided upon. How will each of corresponding activities be taken forward?
<--- Score

19. If you are not happy with the solution, what does it take to extract ourselves from it both operationally and contractually?
<--- Score

20. Are possible solutions generated and tested?
<--- Score

21. What and how are other stakeholders to be consulted and informed of decisions and outputs?
<--- Score

22. Who are the business decision makers?
<--- Score

23. Does the vendor seem to understand your business and your marketing needs?
<--- Score

24. What does the 'should be' process map/design look like?
<--- Score

25. Can the marketing automation solution be adapted to any sales methodology or definition of sales stages?
<--- Score

26. Are the target accounts aware of your organization and solutions?
<--- Score

27. What is the team's contingency plan for potential problems occurring in implementation?
<--- Score

28. Do you really understand how your business customers buy?
<--- Score

29. How did the team generate the list of possible

solutions?
<--- Score

30. Was a pilot designed for the proposed solution(s)?
<--- Score

31. How do you measure the business value of this investment and report the results to the management team or board?
<--- Score

32. How well do you know and understand your target accounts and the individuals you will be reaching out to?
<--- Score

33. What attendant changes will need to be made to ensure that the solution is successful?
<--- Score

34. Who understands the benefits of AI?
<--- Score

35. Is there a small-scale pilot for proposed improvement(s)? What conclusions were drawn from the outcomes of a pilot?
<--- Score

36. Are there any constraints (technical, political, cultural, or otherwise) that would inhibit certain solutions?
<--- Score

37. Are your target accounts aware of your organization and your solutions?
<--- Score

38. What steps are required in developing an advertising program?
<--- Score

39. What challenges does your organization face in developing new products and services?
<--- Score

40. What were the key reasons for selecting your marketing automation solution?
<--- Score

41. How can your salespeople improve selling, negotiating, and relationship marketing skills?
<--- Score

42. Is a contingency plan established?
<--- Score

43. What does your partner and developer community look like?
<--- Score

44. How do you evaluate which platform is best for your business?
<--- Score

45. How to boost your email and marketing automation results?
<--- Score

46. What were the underlying assumptions on the cost-benefit analysis?
<--- Score

47. What communications are necessary to support the implementation of the solution?
<--- Score

48. Is the implementation plan designed?
<--- Score

49. What decisions does your organization face in designing and managing a sales force?
<--- Score

50. What is the return on investment (ROI) for this type of solution to your organization?
<--- Score

51. How does the solution remove the key sources of issues discovered in the analyze phase?
<--- Score

52. How can your organization improve its marketing skills?
<--- Score

53. Is the optimal solution selected based on testing and analysis?
<--- Score

54. How has the solution helped you address your business challenges?
<--- Score

55. How does your organization decide on the communication budget?
<--- Score

56. Were any criteria developed to assist the team in

testing and evaluating potential solutions?
<--- Score

57. How does solution selling fit into relationship marketing?
<--- Score

58. What tools were used to tap into the creativity and encourage 'outside the box' thinking?
<--- Score

59. Are the best solutions selected?
<--- Score

60. What tools were most useful during the improve phase?
<--- Score

61. What are influential macroenvironment developments for your organization?
<--- Score

62. How will the team or the process owner(s) monitor the implementation plan to see that it is working as intended?
<--- Score

63. What is the implementation plan?
<--- Score

64. What tools were used to evaluate the potential solutions?
<--- Score

65. How soon can you expect to see results?
<--- Score

66. How does your organization go about selecting the marketing automation solution that best suits needs?
<--- Score

67. How is your marketing effort for new product development different than your marketing for research results?
<--- Score

68. What are the challenges or risks of marketing automation?
<--- Score

69. What error proofing will be done to address some of the discrepancies observed in the 'as is' process?
<--- Score

70. Is pilot data collected and analyzed?
<--- Score

71. How are you successful in providing training and education for your research and development staff?
<--- Score

72. Does the content creation tool provide guidance on how to optimize the content for search engine detection?
<--- Score

73. What is account-based sales development?
<--- Score

74. How do you improve the quality of leads?

<--- Score

75. Is there a need for a full-blown marketing automation solution?
<--- Score

76. What results can you expect to see and when?
<--- Score

77. Describe the design of the pilot and what tests were conducted, if any?
<--- Score

78. How do business buyers make decisions?
<--- Score

79. How do you improve service quality?
<--- Score

80. How does this solution work; for example, is it hosted on premise or is it a SaaS offering?
<--- Score

81. What are the main stages in developing new products and services?
<--- Score

82. How do you convince your decision makers that adopting marketing automation is the right thing to do for your organization?
<--- Score

83. How can you deliver the insights needed to make informed business decisions?
<--- Score

84. How are sales promotion decisions made?
<--- Score

Add up total points for this section:
_____ = Total points for this section

Divided by: ______ (number of statements answered) = ______ Average score for this section

Transfer your score to the Account-Based Marketing Index at the beginning of the Self-Assessment.

CRITERION #6: CONTROL:

INTENT: Implement the practical solution. Maintain the performance and correct possible complications.

In my belief, the answer to this question is clearly defined:

5 Strongly Agree

4 Agree

3 Neutral

2 Disagree

1 Strongly Disagree

1. Is the suppliers process defined and controlled?
<--- Score

2. What should the next improvement project be that is related to Account-Based Marketing?
<--- Score

3. How will the process owner verify improvement in present and future sigma levels, process capabilities?

<--- Score

4. What is the recommended frequency of auditing?
<--- Score

5. What other systems, operations, processes, and infrastructures (hiring practices, staffing, training, incentives/rewards, metrics/dashboards/scorecards, etc.) need updates, additions, changes, or deletions in order to facilitate knowledge transfer and improvements?
<--- Score

6. Does job training on the documented procedures need to be part of the process team's education and training?
<--- Score

7. What are (control) requirements for Account-Based Marketing Information?
<--- Score

8. What is the control/monitoring plan?
<--- Score

9. Are new process steps, standards, and documentation ingrained into normal operations?
<--- Score

10. Are there documented procedures?
<--- Score

11. How often do you check data and adjust marketing?
<--- Score

12. What tools are available to help your organization monitor and improve marketing activities?
<--- Score

13. How will input, process, and output variables be checked to detect for sub-optimal conditions?
<--- Score

14. Are you operating at a scale to benefit from such tools?
<--- Score

15. Which aspects of consumer behavior does your organization marketing plan emphasize and why?
<--- Score

16. Is there a control plan in place for sustaining improvements (short and long-term)?
<--- Score

17. What are the critical parameters to watch?
<--- Score

18. Are there plans (or considerations) to increase the emphasis on marketing?
<--- Score

19. Do you plan to add any additional tools for account-based marketing in the next year?
<--- Score

20. Does a troubleshooting guide exist or is it needed?
<--- Score

21. Does the Account-Based Marketing performance

meet the customer's requirements?
<--- Score

22. How might the group capture best practices and lessons learned so as to leverage improvements?
<--- Score

23. Is reporting being used or needed?
<--- Score

24. Which standard fields and data elements can you encrypt?
<--- Score

25. Record-keeping requirements flow from the records needed as inputs, outputs, controls and for transformation of a Account-Based Marketing process, are the records needed as inputs to the Account-Based Marketing process available?
<--- Score

26. What are the key elements of a good account plan?
<--- Score

27. How well does your social media plan support your overall marketing strategy and desired customer experience?
<--- Score

28. Who will be in control?
<--- Score

29. Does the response plan contain a definite closed loop continual improvement scheme (e.g., plan-do-check-act)?

<--- Score

30. How do controls support value?
<--- Score

31. Are the planned controls in place?
<--- Score

32. Is a response plan established and deployed?
<--- Score

33. Has the improved process and its steps been standardized?
<--- Score

34. Are there plans to leverage e-commerce opportunities via a mobile app?
<--- Score

35. Will any special training be provided for results interpretation?
<--- Score

36. What objectives should your marketing plan accomplish?
<--- Score

37. Are the planned controls working?
<--- Score

38. Is there a documented and implemented monitoring plan?
<--- Score

39. What controls do you have in place to protect data?

<--- Score

40. Which factors should you reduce well below the industrys standard?
<--- Score

41. Who has control over resources?
<--- Score

42. Carefully observing prospects interactions with your content make sense, and how can you do that at scale across your entire lead database?
<--- Score

43. What do you use (or plan to use) marketing automation for?
<--- Score

44. How do you control the overall costs of your work processes?
<--- Score

45. What are your key performance measures or indicators and in-process measures for the control and improvement of your Account-Based Marketing processes?
<--- Score

46. Is a response plan in place for when the input, process, or output measures indicate an 'out-of-control' condition?
<--- Score

47. Is there a recommended audit plan for routine surveillance inspections of Account-Based Marketing's gains?

<--- Score

48. Is there a transfer of ownership and knowledge to process owner and process team tasked with the responsibilities.
<--- Score

49. How many of your target accounts have complete account plans?
<--- Score

50. Is knowledge gained on process shared and institutionalized?
<--- Score

51. How do you encourage people to take control and responsibility?
<--- Score

52. Do you have a digital online mobile marketing plan?
<--- Score

53. Would a marketing plan help increase participation?
<--- Score

54. Which part of the marketing plan should you focus on first?
<--- Score

55. What are your options if you do not have time to learn a new marketing automation platform?
<--- Score

56. How does the system standardize and match

data to detect duplicates?
<--- Score

57. What adjustments will be required of your teams in order to benefit?
<--- Score

58. Is there a standardized process?
<--- Score

59. Are controls in place and consistently applied?
<--- Score

60. What are the known security controls?
<--- Score

61. Is new knowledge gained imbedded in the response plan?
<--- Score

62. What are the metrics you plan to baseline against in order to understand whether or not the returns of a marketing automation platform make sense?
<--- Score

63. How will report readings be checked to effectively monitor performance?
<--- Score

64. What on-time delivery standard should you offer?
<--- Score

65. Who controls the risk?
<--- Score

66. Do you have the ability to copy a standard report and save the custom version?
<--- Score

67. What other areas of the group might benefit from the Account-Based Marketing team's improvements, knowledge, and learning?
<--- Score

68. What can you control?
<--- Score

69. Is there documentation that will support the successful operation of the improvement?
<--- Score

70. How will new or emerging customer needs/ requirements be checked/communicated to orient the process toward meeting the new specifications and continually reducing variation?
<--- Score

71. Carefully observing prospects interactions with your content makes sense, and how can you do that at scale across your entire lead database?
<--- Score

72. How do you get leads, and what marketing strategy do you plan to use?
<--- Score

73. Who is the Account-Based Marketing process owner?
<--- Score

74. Are suggested corrective/restorative actions indicated on the response plan for known causes to problems that might surface?
<--- Score

75. What does the business want the marketing plan to achieve, that is, what are the objectives?
<--- Score

76. How is change control managed?
<--- Score

77. Which factors should you raise well above the industrys standard?
<--- Score

78. Is your plan to reach out to consumers a viable one?
<--- Score

79. Are there plans (or considerations) to update the brand identity?
<--- Score

80. How will the day-to-day responsibilities for monitoring and continual improvement be transferred from the improvement team to the process owner?
<--- Score

81. Will the controls trigger any other risks?
<--- Score

82. Measure everything. what are the metrics you plan to baseline against in order to understand whether or not the returns of a marketing

automation platform make sense?
<--- Score

83. Are you planning to invest in marketing automation in the next 12 months?
<--- Score

84. What are the current best practices in machine learning and large data to inform marketing decision making?
<--- Score

85. What is the best design framework for Account-Based Marketing organization now that, in a post industrial-age if the top-down, command and control model is no longer relevant?
<--- Score

86. What tools will the team use to monitor the account?
<--- Score

87. Budget: how much money is allocated to the marketing plan?
<--- Score

88. How do your controls stack up?
<--- Score

89. What aspects of your marketing plan can be measured?
<--- Score

90. Who controls key decisions that will be made?
<--- Score

91. Coverage: do you have sufficient data, contacts, and account plans for each target account?
<--- Score

92. What quality tools were useful in the control phase?
<--- Score

93. Who controls critical resources?
<--- Score

94. How is strategic planning carried out at different levels of your organization?
<--- Score

95. Are operating procedures consistent?
<--- Score

96. Has your organization undertaken a formal marketing plan?
<--- Score

97. Are controls defined to recognize and contain problems?
<--- Score

98. Are documented procedures clear and easy to follow for the operators?
<--- Score

99. Have new or revised work instructions resulted?
<--- Score

100. How will the process owner and team be able to hold the gains?

<--- Score

101. What key inputs and outputs are being measured on an ongoing basis?
<--- Score

Add up total points for this section:
_____ = Total points for this section

Divided by: ______ (number of statements answered) = ______ Average score for this section

Transfer your score to the Account-Based Marketing Index at the beginning of the Self-Assessment.

CRITERION #7: SUSTAIN:

INTENT: Retain the benefits.

In my belief, the answer to this question is clearly defined:

5 Strongly Agree

4 Agree

3 Neutral

2 Disagree

1 Strongly Disagree

1. Do you have a marketing schedule?
<--- Score

2. Does your most recent campaign resonate with its target audience?
<--- Score

3. How do you prove the value of this investment?
<--- Score

4. Has there been consideration of any other

alternate service offerings, such as curbside pick-up?
<--- Score

5. What are your current most productive marketing tools?
<--- Score

6. How is the health check score calculated?
<--- Score

7. What are the features of marketing automation that could make a real difference to your business?
<--- Score

8. How does this goal align your marketing team with sales?
<--- Score

9. When should you use a marketing automation strategy?
<--- Score

10. How do you currently segment them and target them across other marketing channels?
<--- Score

11. How do you rate the overall effectiveness of marketing automation in your business?
<--- Score

12. Is your email marketing dynamic based on user behaviour?
<--- Score

13. Do you know the right people to target within

the account?
<--- Score

14. What are the different levels of market segmentation?
<--- Score

15. How can you tell which customers are more important?
<--- Score

16. What happens if half the revenue being generated by sales is new business, and the other half is renewal business?
<--- Score

17. What percentage of leads passed from Marketing to Sales convert to orders?
<--- Score

18. What is the return on your investment for each account-based marketing campaign?
<--- Score

19. How will sales and marketing contribute to the overall strategy?
<--- Score

20. How long can you market to your prospects?
<--- Score

21. Advertising works: what do you really know?
<--- Score

22. How do you align sales and marketing?
<--- Score

23. What are the challenges of marketing automation?
<--- Score

24. What is a common challenge for marketing and sales to align?
<--- Score

25. What marketing programs are you currently running?
<--- Score

26. How does your organization conduct direct marketing for competitive advantage?
<--- Score

27. Who is on your marketing team of tomorrow?
<--- Score

28. How does your organization use packaging, labeling, warranties, and guarantees as marketing tools?
<--- Score

29. What role should social responsibility play in marketing?
<--- Score

30. What is a successful marketing strategy?
<--- Score

31. Do you see marketing automation being a strategic information system?
<--- Score

32. What marketing automation capabilities are most critical to your business?
<--- Score

33. How are you defining success for each campaign?
<--- Score

34. Which messages in the market are getting the best feedback from your target accounts?
<--- Score

35. What types of activity can you track?
<--- Score

36. Does the prize structure matter?
<--- Score

37. How are you currently using your marketing automation software?
<--- Score

38. What are the main benefits of marketing automation to your organization?
<--- Score

39. How do you reach out to the target audience from your target accounts?
<--- Score

40. If you could add new members to your marketing team, in which areas would you hire?
<--- Score

41. What percentage of leads passed from Marketing to Sales are followed up by Sales?

<--- Score

42. How do you know if marketing automation really is right for you?
<--- Score

43. Does the frequency of communication between project team members influence the perceived quality of products or services in the marketplace?
<--- Score

44. What are the things to consider when building a marketing automation stack?
<--- Score

45. What trends are driving the adoption of marketing automation tools?
<--- Score

46. Are your content marketing platforms driving engagement?
<--- Score

47. What content marketing activities do you outsource?
<--- Score

48. Will you be allowed to provide additional marketing?
<--- Score

49. How often is the system updated?
<--- Score

50. Does the marketing automation platform offer

survey functionality?
<--- Score

51. In what ways can your organization divide a market into segments?
<--- Score

52. Can the marketing automation system provide real-time sales alerts over email, RSS or mobile device?
<--- Score

53. How do marketers take advantage of the full Customer Success Platform?
<--- Score

54. How does your organization build strong relationships with business customers?
<--- Score

55. How frequently do you use marketing automation dashboards to track key performance outcomes?
<--- Score

56. What is the future of marketing automation?
<--- Score

57. What are the main things you are trying to get out of your marketing automation?
<--- Score

58. What effect does distribution have on marketing a product?
<--- Score

59. What are the benefits of marketing automation for your organization?
<--- Score

60. Does marketing automation generate competitive advantage?
<--- Score

61. How are you currently interacting with your audience after they complete a transaction?
<--- Score

62. Does the customer want to continue to do business with your organization compared to the competitors?
<--- Score

63. What roles should you select for your users?
<--- Score

64. How easy is it to integrate this software into your organization?
<--- Score

65. How does de-duplication work?
<--- Score

66. Implementation and ramp-up. How easy is it to use the software, and how long will it take to get it up and running?
<--- Score

67. What third-party products integrate with your platform?
<--- Score

68. What are the benefits of using account-based marketing?
<--- Score

69. Do you feel that your organizations marketing strategy is effective?
<--- Score

70. Are your target accounts engaging with you?
<--- Score

71. What is the revenue return on your marketing and sales investment?
<--- Score

72. How do you benefit from Marketing Automation?
<--- Score

73. What can the marketing team be doing to better support your goals?
<--- Score

74. Does specializing in a marketing automation system mean higher expected compensation?
<--- Score

75. What does tomorrows marketing operating model look like?
<--- Score

76. How are you passing new prospects over to sales?
<--- Score

77. How does your organization integrate

channels and manage channel conflict?
<--- Score

78. What is the role of account managers and consulting partners in your customer engagement programs?
<--- Score

79. What is account-based attribution?
<--- Score

80. What topics are your target accounts most interested in?
<--- Score

81. What are your biggest obstacles to achieving your customer marketing/management goals?
<--- Score

82. Is it part of your marketing communication strategy?
<--- Score

83. Which ads work, when, where, and how often?
<--- Score

84. Do you currently have an account-based marketing program in place?
<--- Score

85. What role does content marketing play in your overall marketing strategy?
<--- Score

86. How can you use chatbots in your marketing funnel?

<--- Score

87. Is this the right time to adopt marketing automation for your organization?
<--- Score

88. Does your organization have an account-based marketing strategy in place?
<--- Score

89. What do you think the future of marketing automation will look like in the next few years?
<--- Score

90. Do you segment your sales team by key accounts?
<--- Score

91. How long has your account-based marketing strategy been in place?
<--- Score

92. What are the goals or KPIs that your organization is striving for that are driving this Marketing Automation initiative?
<--- Score

93. Are your business goals aligned across the business?
<--- Score

94. Do you have the right tools to bring people back to your website?
<--- Score

95. Which type of content do you distribute using

marketing automation?
<--- Score

96. How will marketing automation benefit sales?
<--- Score

97. How does the cooperation between the marketing and sales department work?
<--- Score

98. For marketing, what does your target market look like?
<--- Score

99. Which market segments are growing fastest?
<--- Score

100. What are the most commonly used features of the marketing automation platform?
<--- Score

101. What is the role of marketing communications?
<--- Score

102. How does your organization know its spending the right amount?
<--- Score

103. Do you have specific target markets in mind?
<--- Score

104. How (and why) are you using marketing automation now?
<--- Score

105. Has this platform lived up to your expectations?
<--- Score

106. Who in your organization uses the marketing automation system?
<--- Score

107. How do marketing teams maximize customer interactions based on constantly changing consumer habits?
<--- Score

108. How easy is integration of Marketing Automation?
<--- Score

109. What are the practical steps you and your marketing team have taken to getting started on this journey?
<--- Score

110. Is this the right approach?
<--- Score

111. Take a look at campaign performance: are you appealing to the targeted accounts?
<--- Score

112. Does management support this purchase?
<--- Score

113. What is the nature of your competition?
<--- Score

114. How would you characterize your

organizations sales and marketing relationship?
<--- Score

115. What does success look like?
<--- Score

116. Are there niche services certain market actors provide?
<--- Score

117. When it comes to content marketing, should you produce content for everyone or target a particular audience?
<--- Score

118. What can marketing and sales do to achieve the already stated goals?
<--- Score

119. What is your point of difference?
<--- Score

120. What other tools are you using?
<--- Score

121. Why use marketing automation?
<--- Score

122. What has contributed to market grow in the last years?
<--- Score

123. Do you know your ROI on advertising spend?
<--- Score

124. How many target accounts are engaged?

<--- Score

125. Do you have a Marketing Automation system that you use in conjunction with Microsoft D365?
<--- Score

126. What are the options for training and support?
<--- Score

127. Why should you consider marketing automation?
<--- Score

128. Does the system de-duplicate leads on import?
<--- Score

129. Did you move to a marketing automation platform?
<--- Score

130. What are the key funnel metrics for your business?
<--- Score

131. Do you know now what marketing-ready and sales-ready leads look like?
<--- Score

132. What are your goals for your marketing automation strategy?
<--- Score

133. What are your main challenges in marketing automation?

<--- Score

134. How well integrated are your systems with each other?
<--- Score

135. What are the main challenges in marketing automation?
<--- Score

136. How do consumer characteristics influence buying behavior?
<--- Score

137. How is the implementation of marketing automation visible on the income statement of your organization?
<--- Score

138. What does marketing success look like?
<--- Score

139. If one ad is successful, how do you iterate it and make it even more successful?
<--- Score

140. What can you all do to increase the strength and convergence of mail and digital experiences to help increase ROI?
<--- Score

141. What is the Value of Marketing Automation?
<--- Score

142. How do you enable sales to cherry-pick?
<--- Score

143. How can you use paid for digital advertising to boost sales?
<--- Score

144. What is included in marketing automation?
<--- Score

145. Where do clients go or look to buy your product or service?
<--- Score

146. How is digital marketing affecting the revenue of clients?
<--- Score

147. How do you capture the attention of busy senior executives at your customer accounts?
<--- Score

148. Do you track key performance outcomes?
<--- Score

149. What is your digital marketing strategy?
<--- Score

150. Do you typically experience a summer slowdown or speed up?
<--- Score

151. What does your organization do best to connect with its core consumers?
<--- Score

152. How does your business use email marketing?
<--- Score

153. What sales and marketing activities are the most effective?
<--- Score

154. Market research: whom are you after?
<--- Score

155. How is access to the Marketing Cloud Service managed?
<--- Score

156. How does your organization choose the most attractive target markets?
<--- Score

157. What has been the best performing marketing activity in the past and why?
<--- Score

158. What channels do you use for your marketing activities?
<--- Score

159. How does your organization combine products to create strong co-brands or ingredient brands?
<--- Score

160. How long does implementation take?
<--- Score

161. Do you test Lightning apps or Community templates in a sandbox?
<--- Score

162. Where does the customer experience matter?
<--- Score

163. How do you get support?
<--- Score

164. What do you want to achieve from your marketing?
<--- Score

165. Where have you seen the most success?
<--- Score

166. Have you set up dedicated landing pages for your campaigns?
<--- Score

167. What percentage of acquired customers interacted with your marketing programs?
<--- Score

168. How are you going to manage your partner profiling and profiles?
<--- Score

169. How can your organization be a responsible social marketer?
<--- Score

170. When would you use a suppression list?
<--- Score

171. Does your system have support for HTML import?
<--- Score

172. What are the benefits of being aligned with sales?
<--- Score

173. What is the communications mix, and how should it be set?
<--- Score

174. Does your sales team use a CRM system?
<--- Score

175. Should your business adopt the account-based marketing approach?
<--- Score

176. Which factors are you using to build your target account lists?
<--- Score

177. What are the questions you get asked from potential Customers?
<--- Score

178. Do you provide marketing automation certification for your users?
<--- Score

179. How do you reach your customers?
<--- Score

180. Will this product meet your profit goal?
<--- Score

181. Which of the factors that your industry takes for granted should you eliminate?
<--- Score

182. What offers do you have?
<--- Score

183. What are you trying to achieve with each of such tools?
<--- Score

184. What can inbound marketing and marketing automation do for your practice?
<--- Score

185. How do sales and marketing work together?
<--- Score

186. How do you tailor an intervention to a specific market?
<--- Score

187. What are the benefits of marketing automation?
<--- Score

188. What uses do you see for lead nurturing?
<--- Score

189. What is the publics attitude toward your organizations products?
<--- Score

190. Has there been any consideration of a Rewards program?
<--- Score

191. How do you assign a given deal to any specific program, resource or campaign?

<--- Score

192. How can your organization use personal communications channels to influence its target audience?
<--- Score

193. Are any department members working on unusual projects?
<--- Score

194. What types of automation are ready for prime time and which modules are the best candidates?
<--- Score

195. Based on your organizations approach to marketing, do you feel that your marketing strategy is effective?
<--- Score

196. What are the most important factors contributing to account based success?
<--- Score

197. How would you know if your systems are isolated?
<--- Score

198. How does the Demand Waterfall work with Account-Based Marketing?
<--- Score

199. How good are your organizations marketing strategies for your channels?
<--- Score

200. What does, and does not work when it comes to marketing?
<--- Score

201. Does the application have role-based access for customers and third party users?
<--- Score

202. What is the C-suite expecting from marketing automation in the year ahead?
<--- Score

203. How much value do you gain by coordinating your marketing efforts with your sales cycle goals?
<--- Score

204. What are the most important things you have to keep in mind in order to be successful with marketing automation?
<--- Score

205. How many staff are dedicated to digital marketing?
<--- Score

206. What is your brand experience?
<--- Score

207. How does your organization deliver a best-in-class customer experience that meets or exceeds the expectations set by customers?
<--- Score

208. How much time does sales and marketing spend together?
<--- Score

209. Do you use multiple agencies to create marketing materials?
<--- Score

210. Buyer-seller similarity: Should you mainly serve companies whose people and values are similar to yours?
<--- Score

211. How have you selected the categories and tools?
<--- Score

212. Does your organization follow an account based marketing strategy?
<--- Score

213. What should your email subject line say?
<--- Score

214. Is marketing automation appropriate to your industry?
<--- Score

215. How many channel levels are appropriate for your organizations targeted consumer and business segments?
<--- Score

216. What types of marketing technology does your organization use?
<--- Score

217. What are your goals for account-based marketing?

<--- Score

218. How does your vendor continue to support your organization and ensure your success with marketing automation?
<--- Score

219. Does it matter where you sell?
<--- Score

220. On what organizational level should the acquiring of marketing automation be made?
<--- Score

221. What do you hope to achieve by setting up this automation?
<--- Score

222. How will the lead become a sale via marketing automation?
<--- Score

223. Should account-based marketing be a part of your broader marketing strategy?
<--- Score

224. How does your organization build and manage its product mix and product lines?
<--- Score

225. What are the biggest challenges to getting the most value from your marketing automation software?
<--- Score

226. What is the scope of marketing?

<--- Score

227. What is the current state of email marketing and marketing automation?
<--- Score

228. Is account-based marketing right for your business?
<--- Score

229. Do you have a marketing automation system in place?
<--- Score

230. Why invest in marketing automation?
<--- Score

231. Beyond marketing automation, what technologies must every marketer leverage?
<--- Score

232. How are account-based marketing and inbound marketing related?
<--- Score

233. How does your organization respond to a competitors price change?
<--- Score

234. What is the average length of your sales cycle?
<--- Score

235. Which tools do marketers prefer?
<--- Score

236. Who are you selling to?
<--- Score

237. Which variables does your organization use to segment its consumer and business markets?
<--- Score

238. Does the marketing automation system support HTML imports?
<--- Score

239. Should your organization change its business model?
<--- Score

240. Why you are looking for in an online marketing strategy and what you would most like to achieve?
<--- Score

241. Which marketing automation platform do you use?
<--- Score

242. What are the desired outcomes with each account?
<--- Score

243. What do you get for the price you are paying?
<--- Score

244. How exactly do you use a target account list to do social ad targeting?
<--- Score

245. What is right for your business?

<--- Score

246. What types of content are used within marketing automation?
<--- Score

247. Does the system de-duplicate leads from forms?
<--- Score

248. What are the real world uses of marketing automation?
<--- Score

249. What are the primary functional modules included in the marketing automation system?
<--- Score

250. How does your organization differentiate products?
<--- Score

251. How can you truly integrate a marketing automation system into your broader marketing (and organizational) goals?
<--- Score

252. Why would you recommend this platform?
<--- Score

253. How responsive is customer service?
<--- Score

254. Social media including video, can it be used to increase sales?
<--- Score

255. What is your integrated marketing communications program?
<--- Score

256. Which best describes the relationship between your Sales and Marketing teams?
<--- Score

257. Is the marketing automation system being used to its full potential?
<--- Score

258. Do your marketing and sales teams communicate?
<--- Score

259. Adopting technology – have you implemented a marketing automation platform?
<--- Score

260. Who owns marketing automation in your organization?
<--- Score

261. What features/capabilities were most important to your organization when you chose your marketing automation vendor?
<--- Score

262. What situations are best suited for an account-based marketing strategy?
<--- Score

263. Is automation used to achieve consistency in serving customers?

<--- Score

264. Why did you move to a marketing automation platform?
<--- Score

265. Can a sales manager determine which alerts to receive and not to receive?
<--- Score

266. What does marketing automation replace, and what does it complement?
<--- Score

267. How are customer marketing, services communications and other notifications handled?
<--- Score

268. How can you keep your sales team productive in a recession?
<--- Score

269. What is the role of content in entering a new market?
<--- Score

270. What are the advantages of marketing automation to your organization?
<--- Score

271. How does your organization exploit the potential of public relations and publicity?
<--- Score

272. What influences consumer behavior?
<--- Score

273. What are the most effective marketing automation strategies?
<--- Score

274. Can copies of templates be updated with changes to the master copy with your marketing automation tool?
<--- Score

275. What does the customer buy?
<--- Score

276. Are new leads passed from marketing to sales efficiently?
<--- Score

277. How are you measuring your own success?
<--- Score

278. What are your goals/potential wins from an Account-Based Marketing strategy?
<--- Score

279. Do you have web programmers in-house, or do you use an outside organization?
<--- Score

280. Are you also using additional tools for attribution or marketing automation?
<--- Score

281. How is your brand successfully differentiated?
<--- Score

282. What percentage of your target account list is

engaging with your marketing programs?
<--- Score

283. How does web tracking work?
<--- Score

284. What changes in an account-based model?
<--- Score

285. What is your Marketing Automation Eco-System?
<--- Score

286. How much should you use the Internet for marketing?
<--- Score

287. How does your organization choose among potential markets to enter?
<--- Score

288. How does cause or corporate societal marketing affect your personal consumer behavior?
<--- Score

289. Why account-based marketing?
<--- Score

290. How do you maximize adoption in your organization?
<--- Score

291. Why marketing automation?
<--- Score

292. What is your current target market?
<--- Score

293. How does your organization carry out effective interactive marketing?
<--- Score

294. What percentage of your marketing budget is devoted to account based?
<--- Score

295. How might a blended strategy support your top marketing and business objectives?
<--- Score

296. You have another tool to manage?
<--- Score

297. Why use account-based marketing?
<--- Score

298. How does organizational communication affect marketing activities?
<--- Score

299. How do you think marketing automation is positioned relating to the sales funnel?
<--- Score

300. What is the percentage of leads that moves from the first to the second stage?
<--- Score

301. What makes you think your message will stand out?
<--- Score

302. Does the system allow for marketing asset management?
<--- Score

303. How has marketing automation influenced lead generation?
<--- Score

304. Your business will grow; will your marketing automation platform grow with it?
<--- Score

305. Is the business mission clearly stated in market-oriented terms?
<--- Score

306. Does your system provide deliverability services?
<--- Score

307. Which campaign is performing better?
<--- Score

308. Do you see marketing automation mainly as an internal tool or an external one?
<--- Score

309. What is the time frame for integration?
<--- Score

310. Does marketing automation hurt or help customer intimacy?
<--- Score

311. What are the key marketing automation

capabilities?
<--- Score

312. What is behind the rise of the Marketing Operations role?
<--- Score

313. How aligned is your marketing team with your sales team?
<--- Score

314. Which best describes the resources used to perform account-based marketing tactics?
<--- Score

315. How should your organization compensate differently based on the different roles and strategies?
<--- Score

316. How would you track progress in a new market penetration program?
<--- Score

317. To what extent are your marketing and sales force automation systems integrated?
<--- Score

318. Which marketing automation techniques do you currently use?
<--- Score

319. Why is omnichannel marketing automation important?
<--- Score

320. Do you currently use a CRM or marketing automation platform?
<--- Score

321. What sales reports are used?
<--- Score

322. What are you trying to achieve?
<--- Score

323. Are your marketing programs reaching your target accounts, and how much waste is there?
<--- Score

324. How can consumer behavior affect a marketing campaign?
<--- Score

325. How many people are in your marketing team (full-time equivalents)?
<--- Score

326. Does the marketing automation platform provide a way to easily manage recipient subscription preferences?
<--- Score

327. How do you leverage marketing automation with your CRM system?
<--- Score

328. Which selling points work particularly well?
<--- Score

329. What types of reports are used in relation to marketing automation?

<--- Score

330. How can your organization make sure you are selecting target accounts correctly?
<--- Score

331. Are all your automation rules support current marketing initiatives?
<--- Score

332. Who uses account-based marketing?
<--- Score

333. What are the most commonly used marketing automation strategies?
<--- Score

334. Who will manage security of the Marketing Cloud Services?
<--- Score

335. How much employee training have you been able to implement in order to increase product knowledge?
<--- Score

336. Have product sales met expectations?
<--- Score

337. How does your organization respond to a competitors price cut?
<--- Score

338. Automated or email marketing software: which is best for your small business?
<--- Score

339. Can lead scoring be managed in the marketing automation tool and used for targeting or segmenting?
<--- Score

340. Have a list of target accounts already?
<--- Score

341. Are there platforms that are actually automated?
<--- Score

342. How is distribution affected by new marketing trends?
<--- Score

343. Which functional groups are included in account based program execution?
<--- Score

344. What is the lifetime value of your customers, and how can you maximize it?
<--- Score

345. What methods are you using to test your marketing ideas?
<--- Score

346. How does word of mouth affect your marketing success?
<--- Score

347. Do you perceive crowdfunding as a marketing instrument?
<--- Score

348. Which factors did you create that the industry has never offered?
<--- Score

349. What are your marketing organizations key objectives?
<--- Score

350. What type of selling does this strategic account role do?
<--- Score

351. Does your department use project management software to schedule and/or track your research projects?
<--- Score

352. What are the things your organization is doing right to reach consumers in different markets?
<--- Score

353. What information can you see on a visitor record?
<--- Score

354. What are the tactics you used to get marketing and sales aligned?
<--- Score

355. Did marketing automation truly align you with sales yet?
<--- Score

356. What feature/capability is most deficient in

your current marketing automation platform?
<--- Score

357. Why should you do automation?
<--- Score

358. Who uses marketing automation?
<--- Score

359. Is it time to migrate?
<--- Score

360. How are business markets segmented?
<--- Score

361. How do you check the effectiveness of marketing campaigns?
<--- Score

362. Do you consider your account-based marketing efforts to be effective?
<--- Score

363. How will you recycle sales leads that do not move forward?
<--- Score

364. What are the primary objectives of your sales organization?
<--- Score

365. How do you use social media or inbound marketing for your business?
<--- Score

366. Has there been any consideration of a

delivery service?
<--- Score

367. What are your top marketing automation challenges?
<--- Score

368. How aligned are your marketing goals to broader business objectives?
<--- Score

369. Does the marketing automation system have the ability to create tasks for sales?
<--- Score

370. Why did you select this platform over others?
<--- Score

371. Which one statement best describes the relationship between your sales & marketing teams?
<--- Score

372. What is your marketing channel system and value network?
<--- Score

373. Can the marketing automation system send trackable email from Salesforce or Outlook?
<--- Score

374. How much do you spend on each channel or tactic for your account based programs?
<--- Score

375. Is your organization currently using

marketing automation technology?
<--- Score

376. Scalability; your business will grow, will your marketing automation platform grow with it?
<--- Score

377. What types of marketing does your organization use?
<--- Score

378. What do you see as the biggest barriers to adoption and successful implementation of marketing automation for most companies?
<--- Score

379. How do you use your sales team and marketing automation to convert?
<--- Score

380. How will you know the tool is showing value?
<--- Score

381. Do you use marketing automation?
<--- Score

382. What are the components of marketing your organization?
<--- Score

383. How will this technology evolve over the next few years?
<--- Score

384. What percent of revenue to spend on marketing budgets?

<--- Score

385. Are you getting the most out of your Marketing Automation?
<--- Score

386. How would you rate your organizations digital marketing strategy?
<--- Score

387. Do you have a dedicated account based leader?
<--- Score

388. Are automations affected by using enhanced segmentation?
<--- Score

389. What is the hardest aspect of marketing automation for marketers?
<--- Score

390. Do you have any automated email remarketing tools setup?
<--- Score

391. Do you use sales activity lists to keep the team on tasks?
<--- Score

392. Can you account for this transition and how it supports the integration of your marketing team?
<--- Score

393. What are the challenges with membership-based programs?

<--- Score

394. What role does marketing automation play?
<--- Score

395. Can the system run batch de-duplication?
<--- Score

396. How do you want your market to perceive your business?
<--- Score

397. How many users does the marketing automation platform currently have?
<--- Score

398. What are the key characteristics of an account-based marketing strategy?
<--- Score

399. How much of your revenue is at stake, when your competitors outperform you in marketing automation?
<--- Score

400. Do you know what marketing programs are working?
<--- Score

Add up total points for this section:
_____ = Total points for this section

Divided by: ______ (number of statements answered) = ______
Average score for this section

Transfer your score to the Account-Based Marketing Index at the beginning of the Self-Assessment.

Account Based Marketing and Managing Projects, Criteria for Project Managers:

1.0 Initiating Process Group: Account Based Marketing

1. At which stage, in a typical Account Based Marketing project do stake holders have maximum influence?

2. Just how important is your work to the overall success of the Account Based Marketing project?

3. What are the tools and techniques to be used in each phase?

4. How can you make your needs known?

5. Are you just doing busywork to pass the time?

6. What will be the pressing issues of tomorrow?

7. At which cmmi level are software processes documented, standardized, and integrated into a standard to-be practiced process for your organization?

8. Have the stakeholders identified all individual requirements pertaining to business process?

9. Are the Account Based Marketing project team and stakeholders meeting regularly and using a meeting agenda and taking notes to accurately document what is being covered and what happened in the weekly meetings?

10. What were things that you need to improve?

11. Do you know if the Account Based Marketing project requires outside equipment or vendor resources?

12. What were the challenges that you encountered during the execution of a previous Account Based Marketing project that you would not want to repeat?

13. Are identified risks being monitored properly, are new risks arising during the Account Based Marketing project or are foreseen risks occurring?

14. What must be done?

15. What are the pressing issues of the hour?

16. Were resources available as planned?

17. Are you properly tracking the progress of the Account Based Marketing project and communicating the status to stakeholders?

18. What is the NEXT thing to do?

19. Were decisions made in a timely manner?

20. How will you know you did it?

1.1 Project Charter: Account Based Marketing

21. Why is it important?

22. Avoid costs, improve service, and/ or comply with a mandate?

23. Dependent Account Based Marketing projects: what Account Based Marketing projects must be underway or completed before this Account Based Marketing project can be successful?

24. How do you manage integration?

25. Why do you manage integration?

26. Account Based Marketing project background: what is the primary motivation for this Account Based Marketing project?

27. What are the assumptions?

28. When is a charter needed?

29. Where and how does the team fit within your organization structure?

30. If finished, on what date did it finish?

31. Why executive support?

32. Are there special technology requirements?

33. Why use a Account Based Marketing project charter?

34. What outcome, in measureable terms, are you hoping to accomplish?

35. Assumptions and constraints: what assumptions were made in defining the Account Based Marketing project?

36. How much?

37. Why have you chosen the aim you have set forth?

38. What is in it for you?

39. When do you use a Account Based Marketing project Charter?

40. For whom?

1.2 Stakeholder Register: Account Based Marketing

41. What opportunities exist to provide communications?

42. What are the major Account Based Marketing project milestones requiring communications or providing communications opportunities?

43. How should employers make voices heard?

44. Is your organization ready for change?

45. What is the power of the stakeholder?

46. Who is managing stakeholder engagement?

47. Who wants to talk about Security?

48. How big is the gap?

49. Who are the stakeholders?

50. What & Why?

51. How will reports be created?

52. How much influence do they have on the Account Based Marketing project?

1.3 Stakeholder Analysis Matrix: Account Based Marketing

53. Price, value, quality?

54. Who will be affected by the work?

55. Cultural, attitudinal, behavioural?

56. How much do resources cost?

57. How do customers express needs?

58. Who is most dependent on the resources at stake?

59. How can you fill the need to show progress?

60. Alliances: with which other actors is the actor allied, how are they interconnected?

61. Accreditations, qualifications, certifications?

62. Management cover, succession?

63. What do you need to appraise?

64. Beneficiaries; who are the potential beneficiaries?

65. What obstacles does your organization face?

66. Tactics: eg, surprise, major contracts?

67. Who can contribute financial or technical

resources towards the work?

68. Industry or lifestyle trends?

69. Competitive advantages?

70. Partnership opportunities/synergies?

71. Loss of key staff?

2.0 Planning Process Group: Account Based Marketing

72. Does it make any difference if you are successful?

73. Why is it important to determine activity sequencing on Account Based Marketing projects?

74. How are it Account Based Marketing projects different?

75. Professionals want to know what is expected from them; what are the deliverables?

76. Are work methodologies, financial instruments, etc. shared among departments, organizations and Account Based Marketing projects?

77. To what extent are the visions and actions of the partners consistent or divergent with regard to the program?

78. What are the different approaches to building the WBS?

79. To what extent and in what ways are the Account Based Marketing project contributing to progress towards organizational reform?

80. How will you do it?

81. Product breakdown structure (pbs): what is the Account Based Marketing project result or product,

and how should it look like, what are its parts?

82. Have operating capacities been created and/or reinforced in partners?

83. What is the critical path for this Account Based Marketing project, and what is the duration of the critical path?

84. What business situation is being addressed?

85. To what extent has the intervention strategy been adapted to the areas of intervention in which it is being implemented?

86. If action is called for, what form should it take?

87. When will the Account Based Marketing project be done?

88. If you are late, will anybody notice?

89. Did the program design/ implementation strategy adequately address the planning stage necessary to set up structures, hire staff etc.?

90. How well did the chosen processes fit the needs of the Account Based Marketing project?

2.1 Project Management Plan: Account Based Marketing

91. What happened during the process that you found interesting?

92. What does management expect of PMs?

93. How well are you able to manage your risk?

94. What did not work so well?

95. Are cost risk analysis methods applied to develop contingencies for the estimated total Account Based Marketing project costs?

96. Are calculations and results of analyzes essentially correct?

97. Is the appropriate plan selected based on your organizations objectives and evaluation criteria expressed in Principles and Guidelines policies?

98. Does the selected plan protect privacy?

99. Is mitigation authorized or recommended?

100. Do the proposed changes from the Account Based Marketing project include any significant risks to safety?

101. When is a Account Based Marketing project management plan created?

102. Has the selected plan been formulated using cost effectiveness and incremental analysis techniques?

103. Development trends and opportunities. What if the positive direction and vision of your organization causes expected trends to change?

104. Is the budget realistic?

105. Is the engineering content at a feasibility level-of-detail, and is it sufficiently complete, to provide an adequate basis for the baseline cost estimate?

106. What would you do differently what did not work?

107. Will you add a schedule and diagram?

108. What went right?

109. What are the assigned resources?

2.2 Scope Management Plan: Account Based Marketing

110. What is the relative power of the Account Based Marketing project manager?

111. Can the Account Based Marketing project team do several activities in parallel?

112. Quality standards - are controls in place to ensure that the work was not only completed and also completed to meet specific standards?

113. Are all payments made according to the contract(s)?

114. Have stakeholder accountabilities & responsibilities been clearly defined?

115. Are the Account Based Marketing project plans updated on a frequent basis?

116. What weaknesses do you have?

117. Were Account Based Marketing project team members involved in detailed estimating and scheduling?

118. What is the estimated cost of creating and implementing?

119. What are the risks that could significantly affect procuring consultant staff for the Account Based

Marketing project?

120. Which statement about customer expectations is not true?

121. For which criterion is it tolerable not to meet the original parameters?

122. Is there a formal set of procedures supporting Issues Management?

123. Are the payment terms being followed?

124. Are trade-offs between accepting the risk and mitigating the risk identified?

125. Has the budget been baselined?

126. Are Account Based Marketing project team members committed fulltime?

127. How relevant is this attribute to this Account Based Marketing project or audit?

128. Why do you need to manage scope?

2.3 Requirements Management Plan: Account Based Marketing

129. Do you know which stakeholders will participate in the requirements effort?

130. The wbs is developed as part of a joint planning session. and how do you know that youhave done this right?

131. Is there formal agreement on who has authority to request a change in requirements?

132. Which hardware or software, related to, or as outcome of the Account Based Marketing project is new to your organization?

133. Who will initially review the Account Based Marketing project work or products to ensure it meets the applicable acceptance criteria?

134. How will bidders price evaluations be done, by deliverables, phases, or in a big bang?

135. Are actual resources expenditures versus planned expenditures acceptable?

136. Who is responsible for monitoring and tracking the Account Based Marketing project requirements?

137. Who will finally present the work or product(s) for acceptance?

138. Who has the authority to reject Account Based Marketing project requirements?

139. How will you develop the schedule of requirements activities?

140. How knowledgeable is the primary Stakeholder(s) in the proposed application area?

141. Do you expect stakeholders to be cooperative?

142. Does the Account Based Marketing project have a Change Control process?

143. Business analysis scope?

144. How often will the reporting occur?

145. Who will perform the analysis?

146. Who will approve the requirements (and if multiple approvers, in what order)?

147. Has the requirements team been instructed in the Change Control process?

148. When and how will a requirements baseline be established in this Account Based Marketing project?

2.4 Requirements Documentation: Account Based Marketing

149. Are all functions required by the customer included?

150. Have the benefits identified with the system being identified clearly?

151. Does your organization restrict technical alternatives?

152. What is the risk associated with the technology?

153. How can you document system requirements?

154. What are the potential disadvantages/ advantages?

155. How linear / iterative is your Requirements Gathering process (or will it be)?

156. Do technical resources exist?

157. If applicable; are there issues linked with the fact that this is an offshore Account Based Marketing project?

158. What are the acceptance criteria?

159. What if the system wasn t implemented?

160. Is the origin of the requirement clearly stated?

161. What variations exist for a process?

162. Basic work/business process; high-level, what is being touched?

163. Validity. does the system provide the functions which best support the customers needs?

164. Can the requirements be checked?

165. What are current process problems?

166. Where do you define what is a customer, what are the attributes of customer?

167. How to document system requirements?

168. How does what is being described meet the business need?

2.5 Requirements Traceability Matrix: Account Based Marketing

169. Will you use a Requirements Traceability Matrix?

170. Why use a WBS?

171. Describe the process for approving requirements so they can be added to the traceability matrix and Account Based Marketing project work can be performed. Will the Account Based Marketing project requirements become approved in writing?

172. Is there a requirements traceability process in place?

173. How will it affect the stakeholders personally in career?

174. How do you manage scope?

175. What is the WBS?

176. How small is small enough?

177. What percentage of Account Based Marketing projects are producing traceability matrices between requirements and other work products?

178. Do you have a clear understanding of all subcontracts in place?

179. Why do you manage scope?

180. What are the chronologies, contingencies, consequences, criteria?

2.6 Project Scope Statement: Account Based Marketing

181. Will an issue form be in use?

182. Change management vs. change leadership - what is the difference?

183. Were potential customers involved early in the planning process?

184. Will there be a Change Control Process in place?

185. Have the reports to be produced, distributed, and filed been defined?

186. What went wrong?

187. Has a method and process for requirement tracking been developed?

188. Will the qa related information be reported regularly as part of the status reporting mechanisms?

189. Has the format for tracking and monitoring schedules and costs been defined?

190. Is there a Quality Assurance Plan documented and filed?

191. What are the major deliverables of the Account Based Marketing project?

192. Is the Account Based Marketing project manager qualified and experienced in Account Based Marketing project management?

193. Will the Account Based Marketing project risks be managed according to the Account Based Marketing projects risk management process?

194. Elements that deal with providing the detail?

195. What actions will be taken to mitigate the risk?

196. Are the input requirements from the team members clearly documented and communicated?

197. If you were to write a list of what should not be included in the scope statement, what are the things that you would recommend be described as out-of-scope?

198. Was planning completed before the Account Based Marketing project was initiated?

199. Relevant - ask yourself can you get there; why are you doing this Account Based Marketing project?

2.7 Assumption and Constraint Log: Account Based Marketing

200. When can log be discarded?

201. Contradictory information between document sections?

202. What would you gain if you spent time working to improve this process?

203. Have adequate resources been provided by management to ensure Account Based Marketing project success?

204. What do you audit?

205. If appropriate, is the deliverable content consistent with current Account Based Marketing project documents and in compliance with the Document Management Plan?

206. Does a specific action and/or state that is known to violate security policy occur?

207. Does the plan conform to standards?

208. Is staff trained on the software technologies that are being used on the Account Based Marketing project?

209. Does a documented Account Based Marketing project organizational policy & plan (i.e. governance

model) exist?

210. Does the traceability documentation describe the tool and/or mechanism to be used to capture traceability throughout the life cycle?

211. What is positive about the current process?

212. What strengths do you have?

213. Are there ways to reduce the time it takes to get something approved?

214. Has a Account Based Marketing project Communications Plan been developed?

215. What if failure during recovery?

216. Is there a Steering Committee in place?

2.8 Work Breakdown Structure: Account Based Marketing

217. How much detail?

218. Is it still viable?

219. Why is it useful?

220. Where does it take place?

221. What is the probability of completing the Account Based Marketing project in less that xx days?

222. Who has to do it?

223. When do you stop?

224. How big is a work-package?

225. How will you and your Account Based Marketing project team define the Account Based Marketing projects scope and work breakdown structure?

226. What has to be done?

227. What is the probability that the Account Based Marketing project duration will exceed xx weeks?

228. Can you make it?

229. Is it a change in scope?

230. How far down?

231. When would you develop a Work Breakdown Structure?

232. When does it have to be done?

233. Is the work breakdown structure (wbs) defined and is the scope of the Account Based Marketing project clear with assigned deliverable owners?

2.9 WBS Dictionary: Account Based Marketing

234. Are internal budgets for authorized, and not priced changes based on the contractors resource plan for accomplishing the work?

235. Are estimates of costs at completion generated in a rational, consistent manner?

236. Are control accounts opened and closed based on the start and completion of work contained therein?

237. Does the accounting system provide a basis for auditing records of direct costs chargeable to the contract?

238. Are all authorized tasks assigned to identified organizational elements?

239. What is the end result of a work package?

240. Time-phased control account budgets?

241. Are time-phased budgets established for planning and control of level of effort activity by category of resource; for example, type of manpower and/or material?

242. Do work packages reflect the actual way in which the work will be done and are they meaningful products or management-oriented subdivisions of a

higher level element of work?

243. Are the wbs and organizational levels for application of the Account Based Marketing projected overhead costs identified?

244. Knowledgeable Account Based Marketing projections of future performance?

245. Budgets assigned to major functional organizations?

246. Are work packages assigned to performing organizations?

247. Are procedures established to prevent changes to the contract budget base other than the already stated authorized by contractual action?

248. Is all contract work included in the CWBS?

249. Are the contractors estimates of costs at completion reconcilable with cost data reported to us?

250. Are records maintained to show how management reserves are used?

251. Performance to date and material commitment?

252. Does the cost accumulation system provide for summarization of indirect costs from the point of allocation to the contract total?

2.10 Schedule Management Plan: Account Based Marketing

253. How relevant is this attribute to this Account Based Marketing project or audit?

254. Is the quality assurance team identified?

255. Are updated Account Based Marketing project time & resource estimates reasonable based on the current Account Based Marketing project stage?

256. What threats might prevent you from getting there?

257. Has the Account Based Marketing project scope been baselined?

258. Is a payment system in place with proper reviews and approvals?

259. Are multiple estimation methods being employed?

260. Has your organization readiness assessment been conducted?

261. Has the schedule been baselined?

262. Pareto diagrams, statistical sampling, flow charting or trend analysis used quality monitoring?

263. What will be the format of the schedule model?

264. Are enough systems & user personnel assigned to the Account Based Marketing project?

265. Are the processes for schedule assessment and analysis defined?

266. Is the schedule feasible and at what cost?

267. Are changes in scope (deliverable commitments) agreed to by all affected groups & individuals?

268. Were Account Based Marketing project team members involved in detailed estimating and scheduling?

269. Is the steering committee active in Account Based Marketing project oversight?

270. Is it standard practice to formally commit stakeholders to the Account Based Marketing project via agreements?

2.11 Activity List: Account Based Marketing

271. Are the required resources available or need to be acquired?

272. Who will perform the work?

273. What are you counting on?

274. In what sequence?

275. What went well?

276. How detailed should a Account Based Marketing project get?

277. Where will it be performed?

278. How difficult will it be to do specific activities on this Account Based Marketing project?

279. When will the work be performed?

280. How can the Account Based Marketing project be displayed graphically to better visualize the activities?

281. Should you include sub-activities?

282. Is there anything planned that does not need to be here?

283. When do the individual activities need to start

and finish?

284. Can you determine the activity that must finish, before this activity can start?

285. What is your organizations history in doing similar activities?

286. How will it be performed?

287. What is the total time required to complete the Account Based Marketing project if no delays occur?

288. How do you determine the late start (LS) for each activity?

2.12 Activity Attributes: Account Based Marketing

289. What conclusions/generalizations can you draw from this?

290. What is missing?

291. Would you consider either of corresponding activities an outlier?

292. Have you identified the Activity Leveling Priority code value on each activity?

293. What is the general pattern here?

294. Are the required resources available?

295. Is there a trend during the year?

296. Where else does it apply?

297. Activity: what is Missing?

298. Does your organization of the data change its meaning?

299. Resources to accomplish the work?

300. Activity: fair or not fair?

301. Can more resources be added?

302. Have constraints been applied to the start and finish milestones for the phases?

303. Do you feel very comfortable with your prediction?

304. How many days do you need to complete the work scope with a limit of X number of resources?

305. How much activity detail is required?

2.13 Milestone List: Account Based Marketing

306. Global influences?

307. Gaps in capabilities?

308. Milestone pages should display the UserID of the person who added the milestone. Does a report or query exist that provides this audit information?

309. Usps (unique selling points)?

310. What is the market for your technology, product or service?

311. When will the Account Based Marketing project be complete?

312. What background experience, skills, and strengths does the team bring to your organization?

313. Describe the concept of the technology, product or service that will be or has been developed. How will it be used?

314. How soon can the activity finish?

315. Sustaining internal capabilities?

316. It is to be a narrative text providing the crucial aspects of your Account Based Marketing project proposal answering what, who, how, when and

where?

317. What date will the task finish?

318. What would happen if a delivery of material was one week late?

319. How difficult will it be to do specific activities on this Account Based Marketing project?

320. Obstacles faced?

321. How do you manage time?

322. Describe the industry you are in and the market growth opportunities. What is the market for your technology, product or service?

323. Reliability of data, plan predictability?

324. How late can the activity finish?

325. Sustainable financial backing?

2.14 Network Diagram: Account Based Marketing

326. What job or jobs could run concurrently?

327. What are the Key Success Factors?

328. Review the logical flow of the network diagram. Take a look at which activities you have first and then sequence the activities. Do they make sense?

329. Are you on time?

330. What is the lowest cost to complete this Account Based Marketing project in xx weeks?

331. What job or jobs precede it?

332. What are the Major Administrative Issues?

333. Which type of network diagram allows you to depict four types of dependencies?

334. What are the tools?

335. What is the probability of completing the Account Based Marketing project in less that xx days?

336. What controls the start and finish of a job?

337. What activities must occur simultaneously with this activity?

338. What must be completed before an activity can be started?

339. What activities must follow this activity?

340. Why must you schedule milestones, such as reviews, throughout the Account Based Marketing project?

341. Where do you schedule uncertainty time?

342. What to do and When?

343. If the Account Based Marketing project network diagram cannot change and you have extra personnel resources, what is the BEST thing to do?

344. What is the completion time?

345. How confident can you be in your milestone dates and the delivery date?

2.15 Activity Resource Requirements: Account Based Marketing

346. Time for overtime?

347. When does monitoring begin?

348. Organizational Applicability?

349. Other support in specific areas?

350. Are there unresolved issues that need to be addressed?

351. Do you use tools like decomposition and rolling-wave planning to produce the activity list and other outputs?

352. What are constraints that you might find during the Human Resource Planning process?

353. How do you handle petty cash?

354. What is the Work Plan Standard?

355. Why do you do that?

356. Which logical relationship does the PDM use most often?

357. How many signatures do you require on a check and does this match what is in your policy and procedures?

358. Anything else?

2.16 Resource Breakdown Structure: Account Based Marketing

359. Who will use the system?

360. Goals for the Account Based Marketing project. What is each stakeholders desired outcome for the Account Based Marketing project?

361. What defines a successful Account Based Marketing project?

362. What is Account Based Marketing project communication management?

363. What is each stakeholders desired outcome for the Account Based Marketing project?

364. Who delivers the information?

365. What is the purpose of assigning and documenting responsibility?

366. How should the information be delivered?

367. Any changes from stakeholders?

368. Why do you do it?

369. What is the difference between % Complete and % work?

370. What is the number one predictor of a groups

productivity?

371. Changes based on input from stakeholders?

372. When do they need the information?

373. What is the primary purpose of the human resource plan?

374. What defines a successful Account Based Marketing project?

375. The list could probably go on, but, the thing that you would most like to know is, How long & How much?

376. How can this help you with team building?

2.17 Activity Duration Estimates: Account Based Marketing

377. How much time is required to develop it?

378. Did anything besides luck make a difference between success and failure?

379. Based on , if you need to shorten the duration of the Account Based Marketing project, what activity would you try to shorten?

380. What time management activity should you do NEXT?

381. What are the main types of contracts if you do decide to outsource?

382. Consider the common sources of risk on information technology Account Based Marketing projects and suggestions for managing them. Which suggestions do you find most useful?

383. Which skills do you think are most important for an information technology Account Based Marketing project manager?

384. Is action taken to increase the effectiveness and efficiency of Account Based Marketing projects?

385. What do corresponding sources say about Account Based Marketing project management?

386. After changes are approved are Account Based Marketing project documents updated and distributed?

387. Briefly summarize the work done by Maslow, Herzberg, McClellan, McGregor, Ouchi, Thamhain and Wilemon, and Covey. How do theories relate to Account Based Marketing project management?

388. Is corrective action taken to bring Account Based Marketing project performance into line with the Account Based Marketing project plan?

389. What does it mean to take a systems view of a Account Based Marketing project?

390. Is a provider selected based upon defined evaluation criteria?

391. Does a process exist to determine the potential loss or gain if risk events occur?

392. Where do schedules come from?

393. Do you think many information technology professionals have experience writing RFPs and evaluating proposals for information technology Account Based Marketing projects?

394. On which process should team members spend the most time?

395. Why is there a new or renewed interest in the field of Account Based Marketing project management?

396. Find an example of a contract for information technology services. Analyze the key features of the contract. What type of contract was used and why?

2.18 Duration Estimating Worksheet: Account Based Marketing

397. What is cost and Account Based Marketing project cost management?

398. What is your role?

399. Is this operation cost effective?

400. Is a construction detail attached (to aid in explanation)?

401. Define the work as completely as possible. What work will be included in the Account Based Marketing project?

402. For other activities, how much delay can be tolerated?

403. What is an Average Account Based Marketing project?

404. What questions do you have?

405. Does the Account Based Marketing project provide innovative ways for stakeholders to overcome obstacles or deliver better outcomes?

406. What is the total time required to complete the Account Based Marketing project if no delays occur?

407. When does your organization expect to be able

to complete it?

408. Do any colleagues have experience with your organization and/or RFPs?

409. How should ongoing costs be monitored to try to keep the Account Based Marketing project within budget?

410. Small or large Account Based Marketing project?

411. What utility impacts are there?

412. Value pocket identification & quantification what are value pockets?

2.19 Project Schedule: Account Based Marketing

413. How does a Account Based Marketing project get to be a year late ?

414. What is risk management?

415. Are you working on the right risks?

416. Why do you think schedule issues often cause the most conflicts on Account Based Marketing projects?

417. Why do you need to manage Account Based Marketing project Risk?

418. What is risk?

419. Did the Account Based Marketing project come in on schedule?

420. Eliminate unnecessary activities. Are there activities that came from a template or previous Account Based Marketing project that are not applicable on this phase of this Account Based Marketing project?

421. How much slack is available in the Account Based Marketing project?

422. Are the original Account Based Marketing project schedule and budget realistic?

423. Is there a Schedule Management Plan that establishes the criteria and activities for developing, monitoring and controlling the Account Based Marketing project schedule?

424. How can you shorten the schedule?

425. How can you minimize or control changes to Account Based Marketing project schedules?

426. How do you manage Account Based Marketing project Risk?

427. Your Account Based Marketing project management plan results in a Account Based Marketing project schedule that is too long. If the Account Based Marketing project network diagram cannot change and you have extra personnel resources, what is the BEST thing to do?

428. If there are any qualifying green components to this Account Based Marketing project, what portion of the total Account Based Marketing project cost is green?

429. Are key risk mitigation strategies added to the Account Based Marketing project schedule?

430. Why time management?

2.20 Cost Management Plan: Account Based Marketing

431. The definition of the Account Based Marketing project scope what needs to be accomplished?

432. Are tasks tracked by hours?

433. Is a stakeholder management plan in place that covers topics?

434. Cost / benefit analysis?

435. What is Account Based Marketing project management?

436. Are staff skills known and available for each task?

437. Are risk triggers captured?

438. Escalation criteria met?

439. Are quality inspections and review activities listed in the Account Based Marketing project schedule(s)?

440. Are actuals compared against estimates to analyze and correct variances?

441. Have adequate resources been provided by management to ensure Account Based Marketing project success?

442. Have external dependencies been captured in the schedule?

443. Have Account Based Marketing project management standards and procedures been identified / established and documented?

444. Are all resource assumptions documented?

445. Is the communication plan being followed?

446. Does the Account Based Marketing project have a Statement of Work?

447. Change types and category – What are the types of changes and what are the techniques to report and control changes?

448. What is Account Based Marketing project cost management?

2.21 Activity Cost Estimates: Account Based Marketing

449. Specific - is the objective clear in terms of what, how, when, and where the situation will be changed?

450. Were sponsors and decision makers available when needed outside regularly scheduled meetings?

451. How do you do activity recasts?

452. Who & what determines the need for contracted services?

453. Why do you manage cost?

454. Were the costs or charges reasonable?

455. Can you delete activities or make them inactive?

456. Estimated cost?

457. What is a Account Based Marketing project Management Plan?

458. Performance bond should always provide what part of the contract value?

459. One way to define activities is to consider how organization employees describe jobs to families and friends. You basically want to know, What do you do?

460. What is the estimators estimating history?

461. What areas does the group agree are the biggest success on the Account Based Marketing project?

462. How do you fund change orders?

463. What were things that you did very well and want to do the same again on the next Account Based Marketing project?

464. Was it performed on time?

465. Who determines the quality and expertise of contractors?

466. How do you change activities?

467. How many activities should you have?

2.22 Cost Estimating Worksheet: Account Based Marketing

468. Can a trend be established from historical performance data on the selected measure and are the criteria for using trend analysis or forecasting methods met?

469. Who is best positioned to know and assist in identifying corresponding factors?

470. Is it feasible to establish a control group arrangement?

471. How will the results be shared and to whom?

472. Identify the timeframe necessary to monitor progress and collect data to determine how the selected measure has changed?

473. What happens to any remaining funds not used?

474. Is the Account Based Marketing project responsive to community need?

475. What costs are to be estimated?

476. What info is needed?

477. Will the Account Based Marketing project collaborate with the local community and leverage resources?

478. What is the purpose of estimating?

479. Does the Account Based Marketing project provide innovative ways for stakeholders to overcome obstacles or deliver better outcomes?

480. What is the estimated labor cost today based upon this information?

481. What will others want?

482. Ask: are others positioned to know, are others credible, and will others cooperate?

483. What can be included?

484. What additional Account Based Marketing project(s) could be initiated as a result of this Account Based Marketing project?

2.23 Cost Baseline: Account Based Marketing

485. Has the appropriate access to relevant data and analysis capability been granted?

486. Should a more thorough impact analysis be conducted?

487. Have the resources used by the Account Based Marketing project been reassigned to other units or Account Based Marketing projects?

488. Has the actual cost of the Account Based Marketing project (or Account Based Marketing project phase) been tallied and compared to the approved budget?

489. Vac -variance at completion, how much over/ under budget do you expect to be?

490. What deliverables come first?

491. How likely is it to go wrong?

492. Is there anything unique in this Account Based Marketing projects scope statement that will affect resources?

493. What would the life cycle costs be?

494. Has the Account Based Marketing project documentation been archived or otherwise disposed

as described in the Account Based Marketing project communication plan?

495. Is request in line with priorities?

496. What is it ?

497. Have all approved changes to the cost baseline been identified and impact on the Account Based Marketing project documented?

498. At which frequency ?

499. What do you want to measure ?

500. Is the cr within Account Based Marketing project scope?

501. Does a process exist for establishing a cost baseline to measure Account Based Marketing project performance?

2.24 Quality Management Plan: Account Based Marketing

502. Are there procedures in place to effectively manage interdependencies with other Account Based Marketing projects / systems?

503. What is the return on investment?

504. Are there trends or hot spots?

505. Who is responsible for writing the qapp?

506. Is this process still needed?

507. Written by multiple authors and in multiple writing styles?

508. Has a Account Based Marketing project Communications Plan been developed?

509. What data do you gather/use/compile?

510. How is staff trained on the recording of field notes?

511. Are there standards for code development?

512. Account for the procedures used to verify the data quality of the data being reviewed?

513. Were the right locations/samples tested for the right parameters?

514. Who is approving the QAPP?

515. Is there a Quality Management Plan?

516. Is the process working, and people are not executing in compliance of the process?

517. How do you document and correct nonconformances?

518. What is your organizations strategic planning process?

519. Does the system design reflect the requirements?

520. What are your key performance measures/ indicators for tracking progress relative to your action plans?

2.25 Quality Metrics: Account Based Marketing

521. Which are the right metrics to use?

522. What documentation is required?

523. Were quality attributes reported?

524. How do you communicate results and findings to upper management?

525. Is material complete (and does it meet the standards)?

526. Was the overall quality better or worse than previous products?

527. If the defect rate during testing is substantially higher than that of the previous release (or a similar product), then ask: Did you plan for and actually improve testing effectiveness?

528. Is a risk containment plan in place?

529. What percentage are outcome-based?

530. What is the timeline to meet your goal?

531. What group is empowered to define quality requirements?

532. Did the team meet the Account Based Marketing

project success criteria documented in the Quality Metrics Matrix?

533. Is there a set of procedures to capture, analyze and act on quality metrics?

534. What if the biggest risk to your business were the already stated people who do not complain?

535. Have risk areas been identified?

536. Should a modifier be included?

537. What metrics do you measure?

538. What method of measurement do you use?

539. Who notifies stakeholders of normal and abnormal results?

540. What is the benchmark?

2.26 Process Improvement Plan: Account Based Marketing

541. Are there forms and procedures to collect and record the data?

542. Does explicit definition of the measures exist?

543. Does your process ensure quality?

544. Where do you want to be?

545. Are you making progress on the goals?

546. What lessons have you learned so far?

547. Who should prepare the process improvement action plan?

548. What actions are needed to address the problems and achieve the goals?

549. How do you measure?

550. Everyone agrees on what process improvement is, right?

551. Are you making progress on the improvement framework?

552. Purpose of goal: the motive is determined by asking, why do you want to achieve this goal?

553. Management commitment at all levels?

554. Are you making progress on your improvement plan?

555. If a process improvement framework is being used, which elements will help the problems and goals listed?

556. What personnel are the sponsors for that initiative?

557. What is the test-cycle concept?

558. What personnel are the champions for the initiative?

559. Why quality management?

560. What personnel are the coaches for your initiative?

2.27 Responsibility Assignment Matrix: Account Based Marketing

561. Where does all this information come from?

562. All cwbs elements specified for external reporting?

563. What cost control tool do many experts say is crucial to Account Based Marketing project management?

564. Past experience – the person or the group worked at something similar in the past?

565. When performing is split among two or more roles, is the work clearly defined so that the efforts are coordinated and the communication is clear?

566. What are the deliverables?

567. Does the contractors system identify work accomplishment against the schedule plan?

568. Is it safe to say you can handle more work or that some tasks you are supposed to do arent worth doing?

569. Who is the Account Based Marketing project Manager?

570. What is the justification?

571. Are overhead cost budgets established for each organization which has authority to incur overhead costs?

572. What will the work cost?

573. Are material costs reported within the same period as that in which BCWP is earned for that material?

574. Is cost and schedule performance measurement done in a consistent, systematic manner?

575. What are the constraints?

576. How many people do you need?

577. What simple tool can you use to help identify and prioritize Account Based Marketing project risks that is very low tech and high touch?

578. Are people afraid to let you know when others are under allocated?

2.28 Roles and Responsibilities: Account Based Marketing

579. Who is responsible for implementation activities and where will the functions, roles and responsibilities be defined?

580. What should you highlight for improvement?

581. What specific behaviors did you observe?

582. Once the responsibilities are defined for the Account Based Marketing project, have the deliverables, roles and responsibilities been clearly communicated to every participant?

583. Implementation of actions: Who are the responsible units?

584. What should you do now to ensure that you are meeting all expectations of your current position?

585. What expectations were met?

586. Are governance roles and responsibilities documented?

587. What should you do now to prepare yourself for a promotion, increased responsibilities or a different job?

588. Authority: what areas/Account Based Marketing projects in your work do you have the authority to

decide upon and act on the already stated decisions?

589. Is feedback clearly communicated and non-judgmental?

590. What is working well within your organizations performance management system?

591. What expectations were NOT met?

592. Where are you most strong as a supervisor?

593. What is working well?

594. Do you take the time to clearly define roles and responsibilities on Account Based Marketing project tasks?

595. Does your vision/mission support a culture of quality data?

596. Required skills, knowledge, experience?

2.29 Human Resource Management Plan: Account Based Marketing

597. Has the business need been clearly defined?

598. Do Account Based Marketing project managers participating in the Account Based Marketing project know the Account Based Marketing projects true status first hand?

599. Are the Account Based Marketing project plans updated on a frequent basis?

600. Are estimating assumptions and constraints captured?

601. Are adequate resources provided for the quality assurance function?

602. Are enough systems & user personnel assigned to the Account Based Marketing project?

603. Does the business case include how the Account Based Marketing project aligns with your organizations strategic goals & objectives?

604. Is the current culture aligned with the vision, mission, and values of the department?

605. Does all Account Based Marketing project documentation reside in a common repository for easy access?

606. Are issues raised, assessed, actioned, and resolved in a timely and efficient manner?

607. Is documentation created for communication with the suppliers and Vendors?

608. Are the quality tools and methods identified in the Quality Plan appropriate to the Account Based Marketing project?

609. Have Account Based Marketing project success criteria been defined?

610. Sensitivity analysis?

611. Staffing Requirements?

612. Are software metrics formally captured, analyzed and used as a basis for other Account Based Marketing project estimates?

613. Are vendor invoices audited for accuracy before payment?

2.30 Communications Management Plan: Account Based Marketing

614. Why manage stakeholders?

615. What is the stakeholders level of authority?

616. What to know?

617. Can you think of other people who might have concerns or interests?

618. What communications method?

619. How often do you engage with stakeholders?

620. Are there common objectives between the team and the stakeholder?

621. How is this initiative related to other portfolios, programs, or Account Based Marketing projects?

622. Do you feel more overwhelmed by stakeholders?

623. Do you ask; can you recommend others for you to talk with about this initiative?

624. What help do you and your team need from the stakeholder?

625. Do you have members of your team responsible for certain stakeholders?

626. What is Account Based Marketing project communications management?

627. Which team member will work with each stakeholder?

628. Where do team members get information?

629. Who is involved as you identify stakeholders?

630. Do you then often overlook a key stakeholder or stakeholder group?

631. Conflict resolution -which method when?

632. Are the stakeholders getting the information others need, are others consulted, are concerns addressed?

633. Which stakeholders are thought leaders, influences, or early adopters?

2.31 Risk Management Plan: Account Based Marketing

634. Are formal technical reviews part of this process?

635. Are the reports useful and easy to read?

636. Have staff received necessary training?

637. How can the process be made more effective or less cumbersome (process improvements)?

638. Who should be notified of the occurrence of each of the indicators?

639. Have you worked with the customer in the past?

640. Is the customer willing to commit significant time to the requirements gathering process?

641. Which risks should get the attention?

642. Are staff committed for the duration of the product?

643. Are there risks to human health or the environment that need to be controlled or mitigated?

644. Maximize short-term return on investment?

645. Is the process being followed?

646. Are some people working on multiple Account

Based Marketing projects?

647. Do benefits and chances of success outweigh potential damage if success is not attained?

648. Is the customer willing to participate in reviews?

649. Technology risk: is the Account Based Marketing project technically feasible?

650. Is the necessary data being captured and is it complete and accurate?

651. Is security a central objective?

652. Is there additional information that would make you more confident about your analysis?

2.32 Risk Register: Account Based Marketing

653. What is a Community Risk Register?

654. Have other controls and solutions been implemented in other services which could be applied as an alternative to additional funding?

655. What are your key risks/show istoppers and what is being done to manage them?

656. How often will the Risk Management Plan and Risk Register be formally reviewed, and by whom?

657. What further options might be available for responding to the risk?

658. What will be done?

659. What are you going to do to limit the Account Based Marketing projects risk exposure due to the identified risks?

660. What risks might negatively or positively affect achieving the Account Based Marketing project objectives?

661. What should the audit role be in establishing a risk management process?

662. What evidence do you have to justify the likelihood score of the risk (audit, incident report,

claim, complaints, inspection, internal review)?

663. What may happen or not go according to plan?

664. How are risks identified?

665. What should you do now?

666. What would the impact to the Account Based Marketing project objectives be should the risk arise?

667. Do you require further engagement?

668. Recovery actions - planned actions taken once a risk has occurred to allow you to move on. What should you do after?

669. Preventative actions - planned actions to reduce the likelihood a risk will occur and/or reduce the seriousness should it occur. What should you do now?

670. What are the main aims, objectives of the policy, strategy, or service and the intended outcomes?

671. User involvement: do you have the right users?

672. Who needs to know about this?

2.33 Probability and Impact Assessment: Account Based Marketing

673. How do the products attain the specifications?

674. Are the risk data complete?

675. What kind of preparation would be required to do this?

676. Are trained personnel, including supervisors and Account Based Marketing project managers, available to handle such a large Account Based Marketing project?

677. Does the software interface with new or unproven hardware or unproven vendor products?

678. How do risks change during a Account Based Marketing project life cycle?

679. Can it be enlarged by drawing people from other areas of your organization?

680. Can the Account Based Marketing project proceed without assuming the risk?

681. Which of corresponding risk factors can be avoided altogether?

682. What action do you usually take against risks?

683. Who should be responsible for the monitoring and tracking of the indicators youhave identified?

684. Do you have a consistent repeatable process that is actually used?

685. Management -what contingency plans do you have if the risk becomes a reality?

686. Are the software tools integrated with each other?

687. What will be the environmental impact of the Account Based Marketing project?

688. Have decisions that should be left open because of inadequate information on technology been identified and responsibility assigned for reducing the uncertainty?

689. How would you assess the risk management process in the Account Based Marketing project?

690. How is the risk management process used in practice?

691. Do you have a mechanism for managing change?

2.34 Probability and Impact Matrix: Account Based Marketing

692. What is the probability of the risk occurring?

693. What things are likely to change?

694. What are the methods to deal with risks?

695. Can you handle the investment risk?

696. What are the channels available for distribution to the customer?

697. Are there alternative opinions/solutions/ processes you should explore?

698. Does the customer understand the software process?

699. What is the likelihood?

700. What can possibly go wrong?

701. Is Account Based Marketing project scope stable?

702. What are the uncertainties associated with the technology selected for the Account Based Marketing project?

703. What should you do FIRST?

704. How carefully have the potential competitors

been identified?

705. What is the risk appetite?

706. What should be the level of difficulty in handling the technology?

707. What are the chances the risk events will occur?

708. Mandated specific features?

709. During which risk management process is a determination to transfer a risk made?

710. Premium on reliability of product?

2.35 Risk Data Sheet: Account Based Marketing

711. Are new hazards created?

712. During work activities could hazards exist?

713. How reliable is the data source?

714. Risk of what?

715. What can happen?

716. If it happens, what are the consequences?

717. What do people affected think about the need for, and practicality of preventive measures?

718. Has a sensitivity analysis been carried out?

719. How can hazards be reduced?

720. Will revised controls lead to tolerable risk levels?

721. Potential for recurrence?

722. What are the main threats to your existence?

723. What if client refuses?

724. How do you handle product safely?

725. Who has a vested interest in how you perform as

your organization (our stakeholders)?

726. What do you know?

727. What actions can be taken to eliminate or remove risk?

728. Is the data sufficiently specified in terms of the type of failure being analyzed, and its frequency or probability?

729. What are your core values?

2.36 Procurement Management Plan: Account Based Marketing

730. Are status reports received per the Account Based Marketing project Plan?

731. Is the structure for tracking the Account Based Marketing project schedule well defined and assigned to a specific individual?

732. Have all involved Account Based Marketing project stakeholders and work groups committed to the Account Based Marketing project?

733. Are the Account Based Marketing project plans updated on a frequent basis?

734. Are metrics used to evaluate and manage Vendors?

735. Was an original risk assessment/risk management plan completed?

736. Are the schedule estimates reasonable given the Account Based Marketing project?

737. Has a Account Based Marketing project Communications Plan been developed?

738. Are quality metrics defined?

739. Are Account Based Marketing project leaders committed to this Account Based Marketing project

full time?

740. What types of contracts will be used?

741. Is there any form of automated support for Issues Management?

742. Is there a set of procedures defining the scope, procedures, and deliverables defining quality control?

743. Has the Account Based Marketing project scope been baselined?

744. Is there a formal process for updating the Account Based Marketing project baseline?

745. Is the Account Based Marketing project schedule available for all Account Based Marketing project team members to review?

2.37 Source Selection Criteria: Account Based Marketing

746. Is the offeror pricing what is technically proposed?

747. Does an evaluation need to include the identification of strengths and weaknesses?

748. How will you evaluate offerors proposals?

749. What aspects should the contracting officer brief the Account Based Marketing project on prior to evaluation of proposals?

750. Can you prevent comparison of proposals?

751. What can not be disclosed?

752. How important is cost in the source selection decision relative to past performance and technical considerations?

753. Comparison of each offers prices to the estimated prices -are there significant differences?

754. How can business terms and conditions be improved to yield more effective price competition?

755. What is the last item a Account Based Marketing project manager must do to finalize Account Based Marketing project close-out?

756. Will the technical evaluation factor unnecessarily force the acquisition into a higher-priced market segment?

757. How much weight should be placed on past performance information?

758. When must you conduct a debriefing?

759. Do you consider all weaknesses, significant weaknesses, and deficiencies?

760. Is experience evaluated?

761. What should communications be used to accomplish?

762. What source selection software is your team using?

763. Why promote competition?

764. What instructions should be provided regarding oral presentations?

765. How should oral presentations be evaluated?

2.38 Stakeholder Management Plan: Account Based Marketing

766. Have all documents been archived in a Account Based Marketing project repository for each release?

767. At what point will the Account Based Marketing project be closed and what will be done to formally close the Account Based Marketing project?

768. Are the key elements of a Account Based Marketing project Charter present?

769. Alignment to strategic goals & objectives?

770. Are all vendor contracts closed out?

771. Have all unresolved risks been documented?

772. Does this include subcontracted development?

773. Are best practices and metrics employed to identify issues, progress, performance, etc.?

774. What guidelines or procedures currently exist that must be adhered to (eg departmental accounting procedures)?

775. What is meant by managing the triple constraint?

776. How is information analyzed, and what specific pieces of data would be of interest to the Account Based Marketing project manager?

777. Has a sponsor been identified?

778. Who is accountable for the achievement of the targeted outcome(s) and reports on the progress towards the target?

779. Has the Account Based Marketing project scope been baselined?

780. What proven methodologies and standards will be used to ensure that materials, products, processes and services are fit for purpose?

781. Why would you develop a Account Based Marketing project Business Plan?

782. Has a Account Based Marketing project Communications Plan been developed?

2.39 Change Management Plan: Account Based Marketing

783. What are the essentials of the message?

784. Are there resource implications for your communications strategy?

785. Will the culture embrace or reject this change?

786. How will you deal with anger about the restricting of communications due to confidentiality considerations?

787. Has the training provider been established?

788. Who might present the most resistance?

789. What is going to be done differently?

790. How badly can information be misinterpreted?

791. Who will be the change levers?

792. Has the priority for this Account Based Marketing project been set by the Business Unit Management Team?

793. Have the approved procedures and policies been published?

794. Has an information & communications plan been developed?

795. Is there a software application relevant to this deliverable?

796. Identify the risk and assess the significance and likelihood of it occurring and plan the contingency What risks may occur upfront?

797. What work practices will be affected?

798. What type of materials/channels will be available to leverage?

799. Are there any restrictions on who can receive the communications?

3.0 Executing Process Group: Account Based Marketing

800. What type of people would you want on your team?

801. How will you avoid scope creep?

802. Contingency planning. if a risk event occurs, what will you do?

803. How well did the chosen processes produce the expected results?

804. What are the typical Account Based Marketing project management skills?

805. How well did the team follow the chosen processes?

806. What are the challenges Account Based Marketing project teams face?

807. Will new hardware or software be required for servers or client machines?

808. What are the Account Based Marketing project management deliverables of each process group?

809. How is Account Based Marketing project performance information created and distributed?

810. What areas were overlooked on this Account

Based Marketing project?

811. What is the shortest possible time it will take to complete this Account Based Marketing project?

812. What is the difference between conceptual, application, and evaluative questions?

813. Does the Account Based Marketing project team have the right skills?

814. What is the product of your Account Based Marketing project?

815. What are deliverables of your Account Based Marketing project?

816. What does it mean to take a systems view of a Account Based Marketing project?

817. Will outside resources be needed to help?

3.1 Team Member Status Report: Account Based Marketing

818. Does the product, good, or service already exist within your organization?

819. Why is it to be done?

820. How does this product, good, or service meet the needs of the Account Based Marketing project and your organization as a whole?

821. How much risk is involved?

822. The problem with Reward & Recognition Programs is that the truly deserving people all too often get left out. How can you make it practical?

823. When a teams productivity and success depend on collaboration and the efficient flow of information, what generally fails them?

824. Are the attitudes of staff regarding Account Based Marketing project work improving?

825. How it is to be done?

826. How can you make it practical?

827. What is to be done?

828. How will resource planning be done?

829. Does every department have to have a Account Based Marketing project Manager on staff?

830. Do you have an Enterprise Account Based Marketing project Management Office (EPMO)?

831. Is there evidence that staff is taking a more professional approach toward management of your organizations Account Based Marketing projects?

832. Does your organization have the means (staff, money, contract, etc.) to produce or to acquire the product, good, or service?

833. What specific interest groups do you have in place?

834. Are your organizations Account Based Marketing projects more successful over time?

835. Will the staff do training or is that done by a third party?

836. Are the products of your organizations Account Based Marketing projects meeting customers objectives?

3.2 Change Request: Account Based Marketing

837. Will new change requests be acknowledged in a timely manner?

838. How is quality being addressed on the Account Based Marketing project?

839. How do team members communicate with each other?

840. How does a team identify the discrete elements of a configuration?

841. What is a Change Request Form?

842. Who is communicating the change?

843. What are the basic mechanics of the Change Advisory Board (CAB)?

844. What is the purpose of change control?

845. What are the duties of the change control team?

846. What kind of information about the change request needs to be captured?

847. How are the measures for carrying out the change established?

848. Are change requests logged and managed?

849. Who is responsible to authorize changes?

850. What is the relationship between requirements attributes and reliability?

851. Are there requirements attributes that are strongly related to the complexity and size?

852. What can be filed?

853. Why do you want to have a change control system?

854. What needs to be communicated?

855. Are there requirements attributes that can discriminate between high and low reliability?

856. Will this change conflict with other requirements changes (e.g., lead to conflicting operational scenarios)?

3.3 Change Log: Account Based Marketing

857. Who initiated the change request?

858. Is this a mandatory replacement?

859. Is the submitted change a new change or a modification of a previously approved change?

860. Do the described changes impact on the integrity or security of the system?

861. Is the change backward compatible without limitations?

862. When was the request submitted?

863. Is the change request within Account Based Marketing project scope?

864. Where do changes come from?

865. How does this change affect scope?

866. Does the suggested change request seem to represent a necessary enhancement to the product?

867. Does the suggested change request represent a desired enhancement to the products functionality?

868. Will the Account Based Marketing project fail if the change request is not executed?

869. How does this change affect the timeline of the schedule?

870. How does this relate to the standards developed for specific business processes?

871. Is the requested change request a result of changes in other Account Based Marketing project(s)?

872. Is the change request open, closed or pending?

873. When was the request approved?

3.4 Decision Log: Account Based Marketing

874. It becomes critical to track and periodically revisit both operational effectiveness; Are you noticing all that you need to, and are you interpreting what you see effectively?

875. What eDiscovery problem or issue did your organization set out to fix or make better?

876. Meeting purpose; why does this team meet?

877. Is everything working as expected?

878. What is the line where eDiscovery ends and document review begins?

879. Do strategies and tactics aimed at less than full control reduce the costs of management or simply shift the cost burden?

880. What was the rationale for the decision?

881. Decision-making process; how will the team make decisions?

882. Adversarial environment. is your opponent open to a non-traditional workflow, or will it likely challenge anything you do?

883. What is the average size of your matters in an applicable measurement?

884. At what point in time does loss become unacceptable?

885. Who will be given a copy of this document and where will it be kept?

886. Does anything need to be adjusted?

887. How does an increasing emphasis on cost containment influence the strategies and tactics used?

888. How consolidated and comprehensive a story can you tell by capturing currently available incident data in a central location and through a log of key decisions during an incident?

889. How does the use a Decision Support System influence the strategies/tactics or costs?

890. What are the cost implications?

891. Which variables make a critical difference?

892. How do you define success?

893. What makes you different or better than others companies selling the same thing?

3.5 Quality Audit: Account Based Marketing

894. What experience do staff have in the type of work that the audit entails?

895. Does the report read coherently?

896. How does your organization know whether they are adhering to mission and achieving objectives?

897. Are storage areas and reconditioning operations designed to prevent mix-ups and assure orderly handling of both the distressed and reconditioned devices?

898. Does your organization have set of goals, objectives, strategies and targets that are clearly understood by the Board and staff?

899. How does your organization know that its methods are appropriately effective and constructive?

900. Does the supplier use a formal quality system?

901. How does your organization know that its system for managing intellectual property issues is appropriately effective, constructive and fair?

902. Do all staff have the necessary authority and resources to deliver what is expected of them?

903. Are people allowed to contribute ideas?

904. How does your organization ensure that equipment is appropriately maintained and producing valid results?

905. How does your organization know that its research programs are appropriately effective and constructive?

906. Is there any content that may be legally actionable?

907. How does your organization know that its Mission, Vision and Values Statements are appropriate and effectively guiding your organization?

908. Are all areas associated with the storage and reconditioning of devices clean, free of rubbish, adequately ventilated and in good repair?

909. How does your organization know that it is maintaining a conducive staff climate?

910. How does your organization know that its quality of teaching is appropriately effective and constructive?

911. How do staff know if they are doing a good job?

912. How does your organization know that its relationship with its (past) staff is appropriately effective and constructive?

913. How does your organization know that its system for attending to the particular needs of its international staff is appropriately effective and

constructive?

3.6 Team Directory: Account Based Marketing

914. Have you decided when to celebrate the Account Based Marketing projects completion date?

915. Who will talk to the customer?

916. What are you going to deliver or accomplish?

917. Do purchase specifications and configurations match requirements?

918. Process decisions: do job conditions warrant additional actions to collect job information and document on-site activity?

919. Timing: when do the effects of communication take place?

920. How will you accomplish and manage the objectives?

921. Process decisions: are contractors adequately prosecuting the work?

922. How do unidentified risks impact the outcome of the Account Based Marketing project?

923. Who are the Team Members?

924. Process decisions: which organizational elements and which individuals will be assigned management

functions?

925. When will you produce deliverables?

926. How will the team handle changes?

927. Is construction on schedule?

928. Who are your stakeholders (customers, sponsors, end users, team members)?

929. Decisions: is the most suitable form of contract being used?

930. Does a Account Based Marketing project team directory list all resources assigned to the Account Based Marketing project?

931. Process decisions: do invoice amounts match accepted work in place?

3.7 Team Operating Agreement: Account Based Marketing

932. Did you draft the meeting agenda?

933. Does your team need access to all documents and information at all times?

934. What resources can be provided for the team in terms of equipment, space, time for training, protected time and space for meetings, and travel allowances?

935. What is your unique contribution to your organization?

936. Do you listen for voice tone and word choice to understand the meaning behind words?

937. Are team roles clearly defined and accepted?

938. Did you recap the meeting purpose, time, and expectations?

939. Do you ensure that all participants know how to use the required technology?

940. The method to be used in the decision making process; Will it be consensus, majority rule, or the supervisor having the final say?

941. What is culture?

942. What are the current caseload numbers in the unit?

943. What are some potential sources of conflict among team members?

944. Are there influences outside the team that may affect performance, and if so, have you identified and addressed them?

945. Do you prevent individuals from dominating the meeting?

946. Do you upload presentation materials in advance and test the technology?

947. Have you established procedures that team members can follow to work effectively together, such as a team operating agreement?

948. Do you post any action items, due dates, and responsibilities on the team website?

949. Do you brief absent members after they view meeting notes or listen to a recording?

950. Do you begin with a question to engage everyone?

951. Must your members collaborate successfully to complete Account Based Marketing projects?

3.8 Team Performance Assessment: Account Based Marketing

952. To what degree are the members clear on what they are individually responsible for and what they are jointly responsible for?

953. What are you doing specifically to develop the leaders around you?

954. Social categorization and intergroup behaviour: Does minimal intergroup discrimination make social identity more positive?

955. To what degree do all members feel responsible for all agreed-upon measures?

956. To what degree can all members engage in open and interactive considerations?

957. To what degree do members articulate the goals beyond the team membership?

958. To what degree are the teams goals and objectives clear, simple, and measurable?

959. To what degree do the goals specify concrete team work products?

960. How hard do you try to make a good selection?

961. Individual task proficiency and team process behavior: what is important for team functioning?

962. When does the medium matter?

963. Do you give group members authority to make at least some important decisions?

964. To what degree can the team measure progress against specific goals?

965. To what degree are corresponding categories of skills either actually or potentially represented across the membership?

966. To what degree does the teams purpose constitute a broader, deeper aspiration than just accomplishing short-term goals?

967. How do you keep key people outside the group informed about its accomplishments?

968. If you have criticized someones work for method variance in your role as reviewer, what was the circumstance?

969. What is method variance?

970. To what degree will team members, individually and collectively, commit time to help themselves and others learn and develop skills?

971. To what degree are staff involved as partners in the improvement process?

3.9 Team Member Performance Assessment: Account Based Marketing

972. Are any validation activities performed?

973. To what extent did the evaluation influence the instructional path, such as with adaptive testing?

974. Does the rater (supervisor) have to wait for the interim or final performance assessment review to tell an employee that the employees performance is unsatisfactory?

975. Is it clear how goals will be accomplished?

976. What is the role of the Reviewer?

977. To what degree does the teams purpose contain themes that are particularly meaningful and memorable?

978. How do you use data to inform instruction and improve staff achievement?

979. Does statute or regulation require the job responsibility?

980. How do you currently use the time that is available?

981. How are performance measures and associated incentives developed?

982. To what degree can team members meet frequently enough to accomplish the teams ends?

983. What is the Business Management Oversight Process?

984. What were the challenges that resulted for training and assessment?

985. What are the staffs preferences for training on technology-based platforms?

986. Should a ratee get a copy of all the raters documents about the employees performance?

987. Did training work?

988. Goals met?

989. What variables that affect team members achievement are within your control?

3.10 Issue Log: Account Based Marketing

990. Who are the members of the governing body?

991. Is access to the Issue Log controlled?

992. Who have you worked with in past, similar initiatives?

993. Persistence; will users learn a work around or will they be bothered every time?

994. Are the stakeholders getting the information they need, are they consulted, are concerns addressed?

995. Is the issue log kept in a safe place?

996. What approaches do you use?

997. What is a change?

998. How do you manage communications?

999. What steps can you take for positive relationships?

1000. How do you reply to this question; you am new here and managing this major program. How do you suggest you build your network?

1001. What is the impact on the Business Case?

1002. Are the Account Based Marketing project issues uniquely identified, including to which product they refer?

1003. What approaches to you feel are the best ones to use?

1004. In your work, how much time is spent on stakeholder identification?

1005. Why not more evaluators?

1006. Are there too many who have an interest in some aspect of your work?

4.0 Monitoring and Controlling Process Group: Account Based Marketing

1007. What are the goals of the program?

1008. Did you implement the program as designed?

1009. Do clients benefit (change) from the services?

1010. Did it work?

1011. How was the program set-up initiated?

1012. Do the products created live up to the necessary quality?

1013. How well did the chosen processes fit the needs of the Account Based Marketing project?

1014. How is agile portfolio management done?

1015. How do you monitor progress?

1016. What is the timeline?

1017. Did the Account Based Marketing project team have the right skills?

1018. What areas were overlooked on this Account Based Marketing project?

1019. What areas does the group agree are the

biggest success on the Account Based Marketing project?

1020. Key stakeholders to work with. How many potential communications channels exist on the Account Based Marketing project?

1021. Use: how will they use the information?

1022. Accuracy: what design will lead to accurate information?

1023. How can you monitor progress?

1024. Is the program in place as intended?

1025. Are the necessary foundations in place to ensure the sustainability of the results of the programme?

4.1 Project Performance Report: Account Based Marketing

1026. To what degree is there a sense that only the team can succeed?

1027. To what degree are the skill areas critical to team performance present?

1028. To what degree is there centralized control of information sharing?

1029. To what degree does the funding match the requirement?

1030. To what degree does the task meet individual needs?

1031. To what degree do team members feel that the purpose of the team is important, if not exciting?

1032. To what degree are fresh input and perspectives systematically caught and added (for example, through information and analysis, new members, and senior sponsors)?

1033. What is the PRS?

1034. To what degree do team members articulate the teams work approach?

1035. To what degree will new and supplemental skills be introduced as the need is recognized?

1036. To what degree does the teams work approach provide opportunity for members to engage in results-based evaluation?

1037. To what degree are the goals realistic?

1038. To what degree does the formal organization make use of individual resources and meet individual needs?

1039. To what degree are the structures of the formal organization consistent with the behaviors in the informal organization?

1040. To what degree do individual skills and abilities match task demands?

1041. To what degree are the goals ambitious?

1042. What degree are the relative importance and priority of the goals clear to all team members?

1043. To what degree does the information network provide individuals with the information they require?

4.2 Variance Analysis: Account Based Marketing

1044. Are the bases and rates for allocating costs from each indirect pool consistently applied?

1045. Are there externalities from having some customers, even if they are unprofitable in the short run?

1046. Are there quarterly budgets with quarterly performance comparisons?

1047. Are authorized changes being incorporated in a timely manner?

1048. Do the rates and prices remain constant throughout the year?

1049. Are significant decision points, constraints, and interfaces identified as key milestones?

1050. Can the contractor substantiate work package and planning package budgets?

1051. Who are responsible for overhead performance control of related costs?

1052. Favorable or unfavorable variance?

1053. What is the budgeted cost for work scheduled?

1054. There are detailed schedules which support

control account and work package start and completion dates/events?

1055. How do you identify and isolate causes of favorable and unfavorable cost and schedule variances?

1056. Is data disseminated to the contractors management timely, accurate, and usable?

1057. Are your organizations and items of cost assigned to each pool identified?

1058. Are procedures for variance analysis documented and consistently applied at the control account level and selected WBS and organizational levels at least monthly as a routine task?

1059. Are records maintained to show how undistributed budgets are controlled?

1060. How does the monthly budget compare to the actual experience?

1061. Are the wbs and organizational levels for application of the Account Based Marketing projected overhead costs identified?

4.3 Earned Value Status: Account Based Marketing

1062. Verification is a process of ensuring that the developed system satisfies the stakeholders agreements and specifications; Are you building the product right? What do you verify?

1063. If earned value management (EVM) is so good in determining the true status of a Account Based Marketing project and Account Based Marketing project its completion, why is it that hardly any one uses it in information systems related Account Based Marketing projects?

1064. Where are your problem areas?

1065. When is it going to finish?

1066. Earned value can be used in almost any Account Based Marketing project situation and in almost any Account Based Marketing project environment. it may be used on large Account Based Marketing projects, medium sized Account Based Marketing projects, tiny Account Based Marketing projects (in cut-down form), complex and simple Account Based Marketing projects and in any market sector. some people, of course, know all about earned value, they have used it for years - but perhaps not as effectively as they could have?

1067. How does this compare with other Account Based Marketing projects?

1068. Where is evidence-based earned value in your organization reported?

1069. Are you hitting your Account Based Marketing projects targets?

1070. What is the unit of forecast value?

1071. How much is it going to cost by the finish?

1072. Validation is a process of ensuring that the developed system will actually achieve the stakeholders desired outcomes; Are you building the right product? What do you validate?

4.4 Risk Audit: Account Based Marketing

1073. Are all participants informed of safety issues?

1074. Are the best people available?

1075. Does the team have the right mix of skills?

1076. Is safety information provided to all involved?

1077. Have you reviewed your constitution within the last twelve months?

1078. What are the legal implications of not identifying a complete universe of business risks?

1079. How risk averse are you?

1080. Have top software and customer managers formally committed to support the Account Based Marketing project?

1081. Are tool mentors available?

1082. Do industry specialists and business risk auditors enhance audit reporting accuracy?

1083. Are you meeting your legal, regulatory and compliance requirements - if not, why not?

1084. Is an annual audit required and conducted of your financial records?

1085. Do you meet the legislative requirements (for example PAYG, super contributions) for paid employees?

1086. Are you aware of the industry standards that apply to your operations?

1087. Mitigation -how can you avoid the risk?

1088. What does monitoring consist of?

1089. Have all involved been advised of any obligations they have to sponsors?

1090. For this risk .. what do you need to stop doing, start doing and keep doing?

1091. Where will the next scandal or adverse media involving your organization come from?

1092. Are risk assessments documented?

4.5 Contractor Status Report: Account Based Marketing

1093. How is risk transferred?

1094. What was the final actual cost?

1095. What are the minimum and optimal bandwidth requirements for the proposed solution?

1096. Who can list a Account Based Marketing project as organization experience, your organization or a previous employee of your organization?

1097. What process manages the contracts?

1098. What was the overall budget or estimated cost?

1099. If applicable; describe your standard schedule for new software version releases. Are new software version releases included in the standard maintenance plan?

1100. Are there contractual transfer concerns?

1101. Describe how often regular updates are made to the proposed solution. Are corresponding regular updates included in the standard maintenance plan?

1102. What was the actual budget or estimated cost for your organizations services?

1103. How long have you been using the services?

1104. What is the average response time for answering a support call?

1105. What was the budget or estimated cost for your organizations services?

1106. How does the proposed individual meet each requirement?

4.6 Formal Acceptance: Account Based Marketing

1107. Does it do what client said it would?

1108. What was done right?

1109. Was the Account Based Marketing project work done on time, within budget, and according to specification?

1110. What function(s) does it fill or meet?

1111. What lessons were learned about your Account Based Marketing project management methodology?

1112. Do you perform formal acceptance or burn-in tests?

1113. Do you buy-in installation services?

1114. Do you buy pre-configured systems or build your own configuration?

1115. Is formal acceptance of the Account Based Marketing project product documented and distributed?

1116. Was the client satisfied with the Account Based Marketing project results?

1117. Who supplies data?

1118. Did the Account Based Marketing project achieve its MOV?

1119. How does your team plan to obtain formal acceptance on your Account Based Marketing project?

1120. Did the Account Based Marketing project manager and team act in a professional and ethical manner?

1121. Was business value realized?

1122. What can you do better next time?

1123. Was the Account Based Marketing project managed well?

1124. General estimate of the costs and times to complete the Account Based Marketing project?

1125. Who would use it?

1126. Was the sponsor/customer satisfied?

5.0 Closing Process Group: Account Based Marketing

1127. What is the risk of failure to your organization?

1128. What communication items need improvement?

1129. What is an Encumbrance?

1130. What were things that you did well, and could improve, and how?

1131. What is the amount of funding and what Account Based Marketing project phases are funded?

1132. How critical is the Account Based Marketing project success to the success of your organization?

1133. Were the outcomes different from the already stated planned?

1134. What level of risk does the proposed budget represent to the Account Based Marketing project?

1135. What is the Account Based Marketing project name and date of completion?

1136. What could have been improved?

1137. Is this a follow-on to a previous Account Based Marketing project?

1138. What could be done to improve the process?

1139. What areas were overlooked on this Account Based Marketing project?

5.1 Procurement Audit: Account Based Marketing

1140. How do you confirm whether the contracted organization supplied the goods or executed the work as per the quality, quantity and price indicated in the contract agreement/ supply order?

1141. Were bids properly evaluated?

1142. Does the contract meet criteria of completeness and consistency?

1143. If a purchase order calls for a cost-plus agreement, is the method of determining how final charges will be determined specified?

1144. Is the procurement process well organized?

1145. Are there procedures governing the negotiations of long-term contracts?

1146. Was the performance description adequate to needs and legal requirements?

1147. Do the internal control systems function appropriate?

1148. Are vendor price lists regularly updated?

1149. Are risks managed to provide reasonable assurance regarding department procurement objectives?

1150. Are employees with cash disbursement responsibilities required to take scheduled vacations?

1151. Is the functioning of automatic disbursement programs tested by an independent party?

1152. Is each copy of the purchase order necessary?

1153. Is the purchasing department facility laid out to facilitate interviews with salespersons?

1154. Are there inferior competencies among procurement staff?

1155. In case of time and material and labour hour contracts, does surveillance give an adequate and reasonable assurance that the contractor is using efficient methods and effective cost controls?

1156. Was confidentiality ensured when necessary?

1157. Was the award decision based on the result of the evaluation of tenders?

1158. Are there any complaints of the suppliers and/ or end-users?

5.2 Contract Close-Out: Account Based Marketing

1159. Was the contract type appropriate?

1160. Parties: Authorized?

1161. Change in knowledge?

1162. What is capture management?

1163. What happens to the recipient of services?

1164. Are the signers the authorized officials?

1165. Have all contract records been included in the Account Based Marketing project archives?

1166. How/when used ?

1167. Was the contract complete without requiring numerous changes and revisions?

1168. How does it work?

1169. Why Outsource?

1170. How is the contracting office notified of the automatic contract close-out?

1171. Was the contract sufficiently clear so as not to result in numerous disputes and misunderstandings?

1172. Change in circumstances?

1173. Parties: who is involved?

1174. Has each contract been audited to verify acceptance and delivery?

1175. Change in attitude or behavior?

1176. Have all contracts been closed?

1177. Have all contracts been completed?

1178. Have all acceptance criteria been met prior to final payment to contractors?

5.3 Project or Phase Close-Out: Account Based Marketing

1179. What benefits or impacts does the stakeholder group expect to obtain as a result of the Account Based Marketing project?

1180. Planned completion date?

1181. Were messages directly related to the release strategy or phases of the Account Based Marketing project?

1182. What is a Risk?

1183. How often did each stakeholder need an update?

1184. What is this stakeholder expecting?

1185. If you were the Account Based Marketing project sponsor, how would you determine which Account Based Marketing project team(s) and/or individuals deserve recognition?

1186. What were the goals and objectives of the communications strategy for the Account Based Marketing project?

1187. What are they?

1188. Is there a clear cause and effect between the activity and the lesson learned?

1189. What process was planned for managing issues/ risks?

1190. Does the lesson educate others to improve performance?

1191. When and how were information needs best met?

1192. What were the actual outcomes?

1193. What was the preferred delivery mechanism?

1194. What are the marketing communication needs for each stakeholder?

1195. What information did each stakeholder need to contribute to the Account Based Marketing projects success?

1196. Did the Account Based Marketing project management methodology work?

1197. Who controlled the resources for the Account Based Marketing project?

5.4 Lessons Learned: Account Based Marketing

1198. Were any objectives unmet?

1199. Who had fiscal authority to manage the funding for the Account Based Marketing project, did that work?

1200. Did the delivered product meet the specified requirements and goals of the Account Based Marketing project?

1201. How effective was the architecture/system design process?

1202. How much flexibility is there in the funding (e.g., what authorities does the program manager have to change to the specifics of the funding within the overall funding ceiling)?

1203. What were the problems encountered in the Account Based Marketing project-functional area relationship, why, and how could they be fixed?

1204. Whom to share Lessons Learned Information with?

1205. How well was Account Based Marketing project status communicated throughout your involvement in the Account Based Marketing project?

1206. How often did you violate the rules?

1207. What did you put in place to ensure success?

1208. Do you have any real problems?

1209. What are your lessons learned that you will keep in mind for the next Account Based Marketing project you participate in?

1210. How will you allocate your funding resources?

1211. What if anything has been lacking?

1212. How timely was the training you received in preparation for the use of the product/service?

1213. How do individuals resolve conflict?

1214. How effective were the techniques used to prepare you and your organization for the impact of the changes brought about by the product or service produced by the Account Based Marketing project?

1215. What is the frequency of personal communications?

1216. What is the fiscal dependency?

1217. What were the most significant issues on this Account Based Marketing project?

Index

Lightning Source UK Ltd.
Milton Keynes UK
UKHW010910210919
350180UK00011B/542/P

9 780655 913887